T0066701

Ageing: A Very Short Introduction

VERY SHORT INTRODUCTIONS are for anyone wanting a stimulating and accessible way into a new subject. They are written by experts, and have been translated into more than 45 different languages.

The series began in 1995, and now covers a wide variety of topics in every discipline. The VSI library now contains over 500 volumes—a Very Short Introduction to everything from Psychology and Philosophy of Science to American History and Relativity—and continues to grow in every subject area.

Titles in the series include the following:

Nancy A. Pachana

AGEING

A Very Short Introduction

OXFORD
UNIVERSITY PRESS

OXFORD

UNIVERSITY PRESS

Great Clarendon Street, Oxford, OX2 6DP,
United Kingdom

Oxford University Press is a department of the University of Oxford.
It furthers the University's objective of excellence in research, scholarship,
and education by publishing worldwide. Oxford is a registered trade mark of
Oxford University Press in the UK and in certain other countries

First edition published in 2016

Published in the United States of America by Oxford University Press
198 Madison Avenue, New York, NY 10016, United States of America

British Library Cataloguing in Publication Data
Data available

Library of Congress Control Number: 2016944984

ISBN 978-0-19-872532-9

Printed and bound by
CPI Group (UK) Ltd, Croydon, CR0 4YY

*To my parents, Joseph and Evelyn Pachana,
my sister, Joann Somerville, and my husband,
friend, and co-conspirator, Tim Kastelle, all
of whose love and support are constant
and much appreciated.*

Contents

Acknowledgements

I would like to gratefully acknowledge the many friends, family, and colleagues who reviewed drafts or excerpts of this book while I was writing it—many thanks for improving my work and supporting the process…

List of illustrations

Ageing

List of tables

Chapter 1
Ageing, a brief history

The afternoon knows what the morning never suspected.
(Swedish proverb)

Ageing is a subject that is perhaps uncomfortably familiar, particularly in this modern age, with its focus on ways to overcome, thwart, resist, and, in a few but growing quarters, embrace, one's ageing.

Have we always approached ageing with such ambivalence? How has the construct of ageing, and attitudes towards it, changed over time? How have human beings from various historical epochs, cultures, and perspectives viewed ageing? And what impact have these reflections and assertions about ageing had on individuals as well as our broader society? These are the main topics addressed in this first chapter.

Growing older is an activity we are familiar with from an early age. In our younger years upcoming birthdays are anticipated with a glee that somewhat diminishes as the years progress. Our younger selves feel that time moves at a glacial speed, whereas, with advancing years, time seems to flit by at an ever-quickening pace. And late in life, or when a person is faced with a terminal illness no matter what their age, the sense of a finite amount of

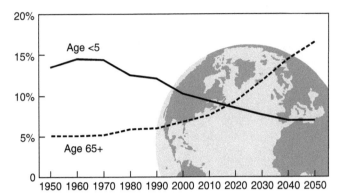

1. **Young children and older people as a percentage of global populations: 1950–2050.**

time remaining becomes acute, and there may be a renewed focus on making the most of one's allotted time in life.

For some, the subject of ageing may not seem relevant, or engaging, or of benefit—particularly since we cannot avoid the process and in most cases, cannot intervene greatly in its outcomes. But current demographic trends make the importance of ageing throughout the world impossible to ignore. As Figure 1 illustrates with data from the United Nations (UN), we are at a point in history where soon the number of individuals over the age of 65 will surpass those aged 5 and under, across both the developed and the developing world. And as this graph clearly illustrates, this is not a passing trend or a blip confined to the Baby Boomer generation—this is the way of the future for humanity throughout the world.

Historical reflections on ageing

Throughout history, in varying locations across the globe, there have been writers, philosophers, and commentators who have had in themselves a more acute sense of ageing, and felt moved to reflect on their observations and thinking on the subject. Many of these historical themes and observations regarding ageing, some stretching back to ancient times, are reflected in modern public discourse on ageing. Indeed some of these themes, such as older persons' roles in society, are a subject of discussion and debate throughout recorded history. It is important to note that although a relatively small number of people may have lived to advanced ages in ancient times, to speak of 'older' individuals at that time generally included those aged 50 and beyond.

The ancient Greeks and Romans had much to say about ageing, its effects, and how to prepare oneself to live well in one's later years. Sophocles (Greek, c.496–406 BCE), who himself lived to quite an advanced age (by most accounts, he lived to age 90 or thereabouts), appears to have weathered his own ageing well. Texts from that time record a story of his sons trying to declare that he is mentally infirm in order to challenge his will, to which Sophocles responds by declaiming from memory a long span of text on which he is currently working. Sophocles also demonstrated in his own life that declines in creativity and cognitive functioning in later life are not inevitable, as he continued to produce well-respected works at the latter end of his life as a dramatist.

The philosophers Plato (Greek, c.429–347 BCE) and Socrates (Greek, c.470–399 BCE) both felt that one of the benefits of growing older is the ability to use accumulated knowledge and experience gained earlier in life. This is a view held in both Eastern and Western cultures, for example in sub-Saharan Africa, where traditionally older persons have been viewed in a positive light, as repositories of knowledge and wisdom. However, the ability to employ such knowledge wisely was not, as far as Socrates was concerned, 'an automatic consequence of old age' (Socrates, *Laches*, 188c). Similarly, in many cultures, both ancient and modern, chronological age is an imperfect indicator either of functional status or social standing.

Plutarch (Greek, c.46–120 CE) recognized the value of older citizens' experience and knowledge, encouraging such persons to take a greater interest and role in public affairs in his treatise *Should the Elderly Run the Country?* This can be contrasted to modern times where, for example, in Great Britain people are excused from jury duty when they reach age 70 (it is currently under consideration to raise this to age 75). Notable modern efforts to enhance older persons' civic engagement include United States (US) President John F. Kennedy's National Service Corps, which was envisioned as providing service opportunities particularly for younger as well as older adults in the 1960s. The Harvard School of Public Health in 2004 made the observation that the Baby Boomer generation 'have the potential to become a social resource of unprecedented proportions by contributing to the civic life of their communities' (Harvard School of Public Health/MetLife Foundation 2004: 8). Coupled with global demographic trends, the potential for older adults to continue to contribute in a variety of ways, including through volunteering as well as both formal and informal engagement in local community contexts, will continue to grow and will be discussed in more detail later in this text.

However, at the same time that many older adults are able and willing to contribute to their families and communities, there are others who require care and assistance at this time in their lives. Plato comments upon support for older persons in society in his book *Laws*, wherein he argues that parents should be cared for and venerated by their children. However, Plato makes this argument precisely because in his society at that point in history this was very far from the case. As is the case with many subsequent writers and philosophers, comments about the condition and care of older persons often took the form of admonishments or descriptions of utopian ideals. In general, protection from abuse in later life has not been routinely enshrined in more formal public legal contexts compared to regulations regarding the care and welfare of children. (However, it should be noted that equally the welfare of younger persons was not particularly scrutinized throughout history until relatively modern times.) A recent example of strong legal regulations regarding the care of older persons comes from China, where the 'Protection of the Rights and Interests of the Elderly People' law asserts that children must care for their parents' 'spiritual needs' as well as their physical needs (the latter being already enshrined in a previous ruling)—including visiting them on a regular basis. This view of the importance of supporting older persons, and particularly ageing parents, stems from the strong Eastern concept of filial piety. Support (or lack thereof) of older adults by children as well as by the state has fluctuated through history and also has varied by culture—again a topic to be explored later in this book.

While Plato and Aristotle (Greek, 384–322 BCE) viewed ageing as a disease, the Greek physician Galen (129–200 CE) viewed ageing as both natural and inevitable. Much lauded as a thinker and medical researcher who was ahead of his time, Galen emphasized individual differences in the ageing experience. One of the first to argue that the brain, rather than the heart, was the location of reason and thinking, Galen even questioned whether cognitive decline was necessarily simply inevitable in old age, or whether it was rather reflective of a disease or diseases that could strike individuals at various ages. He also believed that how one experienced the later years of life was to a great degree dependent upon what the individual chose to do earlier in life. Galen argued for preventative measures rather than cures for ailments in later life. He advised care to be taken in nutrition and also recommended regular exercise, echoing modern research on longevity and staving off disease, including illnesses such as Alzheimer's disease, with attention paid to lifestyle modification.

Plato echoes Galen's focus beyond chronological age in seeking an explanation for better or worse circumstances of the individual:

> ... For if men are sensible and good-tempered, old age is easy enough to bear; if not, youth as well as age is a burden.
>
> (Plato's *Republic*)

Galen was a believer in balance in all things, in terms of not only eating and drinking, but also exercise and rest, as a path to avoid illness. Medicine in ancient times was characterized by a belief that imbalance in the organism, particularly of the four 'humours' (blood, yellow bile, black bile, and phlegm), resulted in illness. Although many thinkers at that time, including Aristotle and Galen, believed that a creeping 'dryness' in the body upset the balance of humours and could lead to illness and decay, it was also widely agreed that this process could be hastened by a lack of balance in the exercise of physical as well as sensory desires. As Cicero (Roman, 107–44 BCE) points out in his treatise *On Old Age*, 'immoderate youth hands on a worn-out body to old age' (section 27). Modern research on centenarians supports the idea that the interplay between genetic factors and a balanced lifestyle (e.g. moderate physical activity and healthy nutrition) contributes to well-being and longevity.

Irrespective of the longstanding idea of balance and moderation practised earlier in life as mitigating the negative physical and mental aspects of ageing in later life, old age as a period of the lifespan has often been characterized quite negatively. Horace (Roman, 65–8 BCE) in his poem on the 'Ages of Man' wrote quite scathingly of the attributes of old age:

> Many ills encompass an old man, whether
> Because he seeks gain, and then miserably holds aloof from
> His store and fears to use it, because, in all that he does, he
> Lacks fire and courage, is dilatory and slow to form hopes, is
> Sluggish and greedy of a longer life, peevish, surly, given to

Praising the days he spent as a boy, and to reproving and
condemning the young.

(*Ars Poetica*, pp. 169–74)

We find a more contemporary echo of this in William
Shakespeare's (1564–1616) famous verse 'All the World's a Stage':

> All the world's a stage,
> And all the men and women merely players;
> They have their exits and their entrances,
> And one man in his time plays many parts,
> His acts being seven ages....Last scene of all,
> That ends this strange eventful history,
> Is second childishness and mere oblivion,
> Sans teeth, sans eyes, sans taste, sans everything.
>
> (*As You Like It*, Act II, scene VII)

The Eastern view of ageing, for example in Buddhist or Hindu
philosophical systems, similarly contends with ageing from a
variety of perspectives, emphasizing over time both positive and
negative aspects of ageing, but consistently recognizing a need
to grapple with the meaning and significance of the ageing
process. By medieval times, though ageing may have been viewed
as harmful and destructive at the physical level, set against a
backdrop of karma (intentional actions bearing consequences),
the maturational process at the metaphysical level was seen
as allowing one to progress from initial student to final
ascetic stages.

In the 17th century, the haiku master Bashō (1644–94), the most
famous poet of the Edo period in Japan, expressed his own ending
life with simple dignity in his final recorded poem:

> Falling sick on a journey
> My dream goes wandering
> Over a field of dried grass.

In his poem 'Ulysses', Alfred, Lord Tennyson (1809–92) offers a view of ageing that recognizes loss while signalling a desire to nevertheless go forwards and explore, echoing sentiments expressed later in this book about successful ageing:

> Old age hath yet his honour and his toil;
> Death closes all: but something ere the end,
> Some work of noble note, may yet be done…
> For my purpose holds
> To sail beyond the sunset, and the baths
> Of all the western stars, until I die…Tho' much is taken, much
>   abides; and tho'
> We are not now that strength which in old days
> Moved earth and heaven, that which we are, we are;
> One equal temper of heroic hearts, Made weak by time and fate,
>   but strong in will
> To strive, to seek, to find, and not to yield.

Old age holds fears for both poets and society. The ancient world shares with the Middle Ages and more modern eras the realization that while a long life is desired, actually achieving old age is met with at best mixed emotions. Cicero describes old age as something which all persons wish to achieve, but which, once they achieve it, they reproach (*De Senectute, De Amicitia, De Divinatione*, Section 4). The early Middle Ages through to the 17th and 18th centuries were characterized by a combination of respect for older persons mixed with pity (or self-pity) for those who had achieved a long life, particularly those most dependent on assistance from others. For example, Chaucer (*c.*1343–1400) describes his older characters such as the Wife of Bath as still active, with the ability to find continued participation and contentment in life. Goethe (1749–1832) in youth wrote more disparagingly of old age, whereas in his own later years he was able to describe old age as a positive time of reflection and activity, as well as contentment: 'That which one wishes for in youth, one finds in old age.' It is not uncommon to see thinkers change their views of the potentialities and drawbacks of increasing age as they themselves enter later life. In his earlier writings, Freud (1856–1939) viewed persons over 50 as incapable of benefiting from psychotherapy, but (somewhat) revised this view when he himself reached that age.

By the 18th century, a greater knowledge about the physical aspects of ageing, including a proliferation of medical texts based more on observed reality than moral inference, foreshadows the gains of the scientific revolution with respect to research on ageing in the century that followed. Attempts were made to identify the illnesses associated with various ages, so that care could be directed accordingly. The increasingly secular nature of European society in the 18th century meant that attention shifted from a focus on the afterlife to how to cope with the last years of life, particularly among those of reduced circumstances. Earlier texts had described the latter years often in terms reflecting the devaluing and suspicion associated with older persons. Bishop Bossuet at the end of the 17th century wrote of old age as 'ordinarily...soiled with the filth of avarice', echoing sentiments which go back to pre-Christian times. By contrast, at the end of the 18th and the beginning of the 19th centuries, the new Age of Enlightenment is reflected in J.H. Meister's writing of the continuing creativity of older persons, the pleasures of grandparenthood, and, most significantly, that the current age, with its progress and ambitions, belonged equally to persons of all ages.

Unfortunately events in many parts of the world, but particularly the developing world, have changed the nature of the ageing experience across cultures. Regional conflicts, migration to flee conflict or economic hardship, rapid modernization conflicting with traditional societal norms, and the effects of disease, particularly the impact of HIV/AIDS in sub-Saharan Africa, have had differential impacts on older persons. Increasingly, global surveys of ageing are expanding knowledge of the experiences of older adults, but for some populations, including indigenous peoples, isolated populations, and sub-Saharan Africa and parts of the Middle East, it remains unknown to what extent older persons are able to participate in the progress and ambitions of the modern age alluded to in the previous paragraph.

There is a range of contemporary writings on ageing, sometimes positive or meditative, sometimes forceful and directive, as Welsh poet Dylan Thomas's (1914–53) lines from his famous poem illustrate:

> Do not go gentle into that good night,
> Old age should burn and rave at close of day…

From the ancient world to the modern there are conflicting views with respect to ageing. On the one hand, there is recognition of the potential benefits that may accrue with ageing, and the good, even noble, characteristics associated with increasing age—wisdom, experience, continuing vigour and engagement with life. At the same time, within individuals or even societies, age is viewed with fear and dread. Ageing from this perspective is tied to incipient declines in mental, social, and physical functioning, with the loss of friends and family over time decried, and increasing societal irrelevance met with despair. Individual persons as well as the many scientific disciplines and societies which have at some stage focused on ageing have also displayed this dualism, with at times greater or lesser attention paid to the virtues and drawbacks associated with ageing and a long life. This conflict is reflected in Dewey's paradox of ageing, which in effect states that while we value maturity yet we fail to value ageing.

Being able to better understand and cope with individual ageing as well as an ageing society is critical, particularly as the human lifespan continues to lengthen worldwide.

Historical trends in longevity and lifespan

Most people have an idea that 'lifespan' refers to how long a person lives, and that how long individuals are living has increased over time. However, 'life expectancy' (a prediction based mostly on actuarial tables and often incorrect) differs from the concept of either usual or maximum lifespan. Life expectancy is calculated by averaging the age at death for all persons who have been born in a country, including those who have lived into old age and those who died shortly after birth; those who died in early adulthood; those who died by trauma or disease; and so forth. (See Table 1 for life expectancy figures across various regions of the world.) Lifespan, by contrast, refers to cumulative records of the span of years individuals have lived that have not been averaged out. Maximum lifespan refers to the purported maximum lifespan humans are currently believed to be able to achieve based on current biological knowledge, and is better thought of as an upper limit to survival rather than an average of the age to which one

Table 1 Life expectancy at birth and at age 60 by WHO region, 2009

WHO region	Life expectancy at birth (years) male/female	Life expectancy at 60 years (years) male/female
World	66/71	18/21
Africa	52/56	14/16
Americas	73/79	21/24
Eastern Mediterranean	64/67	16/18
Europe	71/79	19/23
South East Asia	64/67	15/18
Western Pacific	72/77	19/22

WHO (2011). *World Health Statistics*. Geneva: WHO. With permission from John Beard.

might live. Modern *gerontology*, the scientific study of ageing, places the theoretical limits of ageing at approximately age 120.

Precisely how long *are* people living, across various historical time periods and societies? Due to the fact that throughout history, including in modern times, there are so many persons who die very shortly after birth and before the age of 1, it is arguably better to calculate life expectancies by looking at populations no longer in early childhood, and this also will help us to better understand factors affecting lifespan. For example, in Roman times life expectancy taken from birth was around 21 years, whereas taken from age 5 it increased to 42 years. This pattern is repeated in various societies and cultures, where historically very young children have experienced high mortality due to several factors including disease, malnutrition, and poor hygiene. High rates of *morbidity* (illness) and *mortality* (death) in young children have only changed relatively recently, and these changes are a phenomenon still in progress throughout most of the developing world.

Although the relatively old age recorded for the philosophers and writers cited earlier (e.g. Plato and Sophocles) appears accurate, longevity, and moreover ideas about longevity, have fluctuated over time. In literature, for example in the Bible, we see testaments about people living to great ages. For example, Adam is said to have lived for 930 years, Noah for 950 years, and Methuselah (appropriately) for 969 years. Many cultures, including ancient Greece, contain stories or myths about the ages of long-lived individuals or groups in the distant past, with a progressive trend towards shorter lifespans driven by increasingly decadent 'modern' lifestyles. Such stories of extreme lifespan in ancient times are archetypal of an antediluvian theme, returned to periodically by writers throughout history.

The antediluvian theme can be contrasted with the hyperborean theme (literally 'hyper' meaning 'beyond', and 'boreas' meaning 'the North Wind'), originally about long-lived cultures that existed in the extreme northern lands of Europe. A wide range of explorers, from Alexander the Great to Ponce de Leon, searched widely but in vain for the fabled Fountain of Youth. These stories have resonance today in literature and films about mythical places of long life, for example Shangri-La as portrayed in James Hilton's book *Lost Horizon* (1933), which exemplifies the modern search for answers about living longer among isolated peoples with great longevity. A popular contemporary take on the hyperborean theme is reflected in National Geographic's exploration with author Dan Buettner and longevity scientists of places around the world (so-called 'Blue Zones') where people are said to live very long lives. Indeed, some research points to people surviving to age 100 ten times more often in Blue Zones than in other places.

Throughout history, people have sought to extend longevity, or years of life lived, ideally avoiding illness and disease. In both antediluvian and hyperboreal stories, people either lived forever or with greatly expanded lifespans, into the hundreds of years. Often the means to such long life were quite creative. For example, in many societies, *gerocomy*, the belief that intercourse with younger women could delay or even reverse ageing, was common. And today, unfortunately, this belief persists in sub-Saharan Africa, where sex with younger women in pursuit of health benefits has contributed to the spread of HIV and AIDS.

Although the modern perception may be that achieving a great age is a relatively recent phenomena, there is ample evidence throughout history that some percentage of persons have always achieved what we would today characterize as a 'ripe old age'. For example, in ancient Greece and the Roman Empire, roughly 6–8 per cent of the population would have lived to age 60+, with perhaps 3 per cent living to age 80+ (Parkin 2003: from Coale-Demeny Model Life Tables). Similarly in medieval times those over age 60 constituted roughly 8 per cent of the population at any given time, although this figure could rise to roughly double that in the aftermath of plagues, as these events killed proportionately more younger than older persons. In the 17th and 18th centuries, first in northern Europe and later more widely, the number of persons over age 60 began to slowly increase as a proportion of the population, to around 10 per cent on average. Gains in longevity at this point in history were due to a range of societal advances. These included improved storage and transportation of food, and improvements in well-being due to social welfare programmes and other attempts to ease the plight of the poor (for example, the later rise of public service pensions in Britain, France, and Germany).

However, the modern era is characterized by the high percentage of older adults in some countries, forming 20 to 25 per cent of the population, with rates of births lagging behind deaths in many of these nations. Modern gains in longevity in the 19th and 20th centuries are a product of continued gains in sanitation, food safety and abundance, and societal programmes to support persons in reduced circumstances, coupled with medical advances in the prevention and treatment of disease. This then is a new and interesting point in history, where significant numbers of older adults are contributing to and influencing society, through their actions and their sheer numbers.

Of countries with over ten million inhabitants as of 2002, projections are that at least ten will have close to or over 30 per cent of their population aged 60+ by 2025; these include Japan, Italy, Germany, Greece, Spain, Belgium, the United Kingdom, the Netherlands, France, and Canada. Also by 2025, China is expected to have nearly 300 million people over age 60, with India projected to have the second highest absolute number of such persons (close to 170 million).

Moreover, societies are reaching the point where significant portions of their populations are over the age of 65 at varying rates.

For example, whereas France as a country took nearly 120 years to double its number of persons over age 65 as a percentage of the overall population (from 7 to 14 per cent), South Korea, one of the fastest ageing countries in the world, will achieve the same milestone in less than twenty years. Such rapid growth in numbers of older persons within a country or region has consequences for how generations interact, how states plan for retirement and a social safety net, and the expectations of the roles of older persons in the family and wider society. When a society adapts to such demographic changes slowly, persons can adjust gradually at the family and community levels, whereas in the face of more rapid shifts in demographic distributions, changes to social structures may shift more abruptly, with the potential for an uneasy transition. Today many parts of the developing world are experiencing such rapid shifts in increasing numbers of older persons as a proportion of the population, due to health and medical advances. In these countries, challenges to infrastructure, health services, and economic safeguards for older persons are often particularly acute.

Since some proportion of people were living to age 60, 70, and beyond even in ancient times, traditionally old age has been said to start somewhere between ages 49 and 70, and most systems of breaking the lifespan into segments have included some version of young, middle, and old age, often broken down more finely. For example, in France historically there is a division between the 'first age' (youth), the 'second age' (maturity), the 'third age' (the period after children have been raised), and a final 'fourth age' (old age). The University of the Third Age (U3A) international movement is inspired by the French 'troisième age' to encourage those in this period of life to pursue self-learning and enrichment, organized by and for similar-aged peers. U3A operates in France, where it originated, as well as in many other European countries; it also has a virtual presence (vU3A) aimed particularly at those who, due to health problems or other barriers, cannot attend U3A meetings.

Much less optimistic is the 16th-century German description of the decades of life:

10 years—a child
20 years—youth
30 years—a man
40 years—standing still
50 years—settled and prosperous
60 years—departing
70 years—protect your soul
80 years—the world's fool
90 years—the scorn of children
100 years—God have mercy

In modern gerontology there is a distinction made between the 'young-old' (aged 65–74), 'old-old' (aged 75–84), and 'oldest old' (aged 85+). There is renewed interest in studying this latter group, particularly as globally, longevity increases on average by about three months per year, or about five hours per day. The numbers of centenarian studies (examining those aged 100+) and supercentenarian studies (focused on those aged 110+) are increasing internationally, and have as their subject of inquiry everything from biological markers of ageing to social and political activity in these individuals.

Historically, as societies experienced decreased birth rates and increased numbers of older adults surviving for longer, a shift occurred in the composition of the population. What might previously have been described as a population pyramid, with large numbers of younger persons at the base, narrowing towards a peak of fewer persons at later ages, now began to shift in shape. In modern times this shift has accelerated further, with the population pyramid now more resembling a rectangle, with more equal numbers of persons in the age bands from birth to old age.

The discipline of cross-species studies of longevity is one of the newer fields of study to contribute to the science of ageing. Many scientists, beginning with Darwin in his *On the Origin of Species* in 1859, observed that various species live for greater or lesser periods of time. Ageing differs dramatically between species. Some whale species live over 200 years, as do some species of koi fish, while many mammals live less than one year, and some insect species live for mere days.

While many theories have been espoused to account for varying lifespans within the animal kingdom, such as metabolic theories influencing longevity, there is still much debate in this field. Even today, scientific theories of ageing, explored further in Chapter 2 on biological ageing, cannot fully account for the diversity of lifespans observed in nature. More research is required in this area before we can unravel the reasons for this variation in lifespan across species.

Factors influencing life expectancy and ageing

Life expectancy in humans over time has been affected adversely by historical events, such as wars and pandemics. The bubonic plague in the 14th century, and the flu pandemic of 1918, are examples of widespread disease outbreaks which impacted life expectancy at those points in history. Many armed conflicts have severely impacted the societies in which they have been fought, influencing population distributions for many years post-conflict. For example, many wars disproportionately claim young male lives, and in the Paraguayan War in the late 19th century, estimates are that as much as 70 per cent of the adult male population of Paraguay perished.

Occupation influences mortality, and is tied in many cases to gender. Throughout history and including modern times, men have traditionally taken on more hazardous occupations than women. However, the impact of an occupation on ageing processes, particularly in the pre-industrial age, could be marked. For example, sailors and miners, predominantly male, suffered a variety of ailments (such as lung disease and scurvy) that curtailed their lifespans, often severely. An occupation such as lacemaking, predominantly pursued by women, could lead to premature blindness and loss of function due to arthritic fingers. On the other hand, those in religious orders, whether male or female, generally enjoyed relatively longer lives compared to peers. The generally homogenous and gentle conditions favourable to ageing offered by organized religious orders were used by David Snowdon, an epidemiologist and neurologist at the University of Kentucky, whose longitudinal studies of ageing nuns afforded insights into the effects of early life influences on ageing and risk of dementia.

Gender itself plays an important and only partially understood role in mortality; up until medical advances in the 20th century greatly reduced death in childbirth, women's life expectancies were lower than those of men. At the current time, in all countries where such data are available, women outlive men. A recent study by Beltran-Sanchez and colleagues in 2015, using data from thirteen developed countries, suggests that increased male risk of cardiovascular disease in those born after 1900 is one modern driver of this phenomenon, with the excess male mortality specifically located in the 50–70 age group. Having enjoyed greater longevity worldwide for many decades, women now represent 90 per cent of supercentenarians. With the exception of birds, for almost all of the species of animals that have been studied, females are longer lived than males.

Unfortunately, women also report greater physical and mental health symptoms than men in later life (and in fact throughout their lifespan), and although some of the data are mixed, most research from a variety of nations supports this assertion. Why might this be the case? The most common explanations of women's health disadvantage reflect biological differences between the sexes, different patterns of illness and health behaviour reporting, physicians' diagnostic patterns, and differential healthcare access, treatment, and use.

Despite their greater longevity, women in later life (and arguably women at all points in their lifespan) have not been well-regarded historically. Many of the texts, treatises, and pieces of literature which comment on ageing in the ancient world through to the Middle Ages often refer exclusively to men. Some of this can be attributed to the fact that, for example, as military service or government offices were for the most part only open to men, women were not mentioned specifically in official records. From Roman times onwards, older women were at best marginalized within society, and at worst cast as ineffectual, described by many authors as debased in thought and behaviour by ungovernable desires (e.g. for sex or alcohol).

Although until recently women in all social classes experienced higher mortality due to deaths in childbirth, other circumstances pertaining to women's roles in society also contributed to historically lower mortality for females. While men disproportionately were involved in individual or communal conflicts, women had a disproportionate responsibility for caring for the sick and injured (a circumstance which remains today) and, thus, particularly before the advent of modern medicine, they were exposed to illness and infection at higher rates than men.

The age gap between heterosexual partners in ancient times through the Middle Ages and even into more modern eras (with men tending to marry women younger than themselves) contributed to the relatively higher proportion of widows to widowers, rather than this being a consequence of women's greater longevity. In antiquity and through the Middle Ages, and to a lesser extent into more modern times, widowers tended to remarry at a much higher rate than widows, and to remarry relatively younger spouses. The social norm of women traditionally marrying older men, even today, tends to mitigate against higher rates of remarriage for older women. However, many older women are also cautious of remarrying later in life, particularly if they experienced intense caregiving responsibilities in their prior relationship.

Globally, mortality rates still vary widely. Japan, the longest-lived society, has both males and females on average living past the age of 90. Life expectancy at birth is over 80 in more than thirty countries. In contrast, in sub-Saharan African countries, life expectancy may range from mid-30s to mid-40s due to both armed conflict and AIDS and other diseases. The UN in 2002 estimated that if HIV/AIDS did not exist, lifespans in South Africa, Botswana, and Zimbabwe would be around 70 today.

However, longevity can also vary greatly even within a society. For example, life expectancy for children born in 2014 in the UK ranges from 67 to 105, depending on where they live. And in Glasgow, this disparity in life expectancy is one of the highest in the world, with males in the economically deprived Calton area expected on average to live to 54, while males living in more affluent Lenzie on average live to 82.

Medical advances as well as public health advances have had a great impact on raising life expectancy globally during the 20th century. The simple act of practitioners washing their hands when delivering medical care has had a disproportionately large impact on mortality by curtailing the spread of pathogens during surgery and childbirth. In the past, public health services contributed to programmes such as vaccination efforts, which had a large impact on decreasing acute illnesses. Now that the incidence of many acute (severe, sudden onset) illnesses experienced relatively early in life, such as polio, has decreased dramatically, chronic (long-developing) diseases contribute proportionately more to disability and death in most societies. Thus public health efforts globally have shifted at least somewhat in response to the ageing of societies by placing increasing focus on education about chronic illnesses of later life, such as diabetes, cardiovascular conditions, and cancer.

Today life expectancy plays an increasingly important role in public policy. For example, life expectancy is one of the factors used in the calculation of the Human Development Index (HDI) of nations, along with education and standard of living. Increasing life expectancies contribute to the rising median age of countries, with social and economic impacts of, for example, an ageing workforce. And in both the developed and the developing world, rising numbers of older persons find themselves living in poverty. While poverty has often been the fate of older persons throughout history, medical advances have increased the numbers of older persons reaching advanced ages who have to cope with such consequences of biological ageing. Physical and biological aspects of ageing are the focus of Chapter 2.

Chapter 2
Physical and biological aspects of ageing

> Every man desires to live long, but no man would be old.
>
> (Jonathan Swift (1667-1745), *Thoughts on*
> *Various Subjects*)

The previous chapter discussed the constructs of ageing
and longevity across historical time. The current chapter moves
into a discussion of biological and physical aspects of ageing,
how these influence longevity, and particular physical
disorders commonly experienced at the end of life, including
dementia.

The WHO definition of health states that health goes beyond
physical health to encompass 'a complete state of physical, mental
and social well-being, and not merely the absence of disease
or infirmity' (WHO 1948). Thus health is conceptualized as
more holistic than a strictly medical definition, and this has
implications for ageing. It is important to note that while in this
chapter biological aspects of health and ageing are considered,
a broader framework of health should be borne in mind, one
which encompasses psychological and sociocultural aspects of
health and ageing.

Primary and secondary ageing, and heterogeneity in later life

Changes in the organism on a biological, psychological, and social level, evolving primarily as a result of the passage of chronological time, are the definition of *primary ageing*. Primary ageing changes include wear and tear on organs as a result of their use over time, and we can do very little to slow or reverse such changes. Examples of changes in human biology as a function of primary ageing include decreased production of neurotransmitters, the chemical messengers of the brain, as well as a decreased sensitivity of neural receptors in the brain to receive such messages (see Table 2 for more such examples of primary and secondary ageing effects). Note that the magnitude of declines in such primary ageing changes are relatively stable across the lifespan, but their cumulative effect may become more noticeable as we age.

Examples of primary and secondary ageing effects on biological ageing

Secondary ageing is, by contrast, the term for changes in the organism that are a result of a disease process, as well as damage

Table 2 Changes due to primary and secondary ageing: physical/biological

Primary ageing changes	Secondary ageing changes
Visual acuity, particularly for near distance, declines	Macular degeneration
Muscle mass and bone density decline	Disability as a result of injury
Hearing loss	Osteoporosis
Decreased resistance to infections	Coronary disease, type II diabetes and other forms of chronic disease
Menopause	Cancer

to the organism due to life events, such as experience of head trauma; and the results of lifestyle choices, such as diet and exercise. Examples of secondary ageing effects include the development of cardiac disease or Alzheimer's disease. Whereas changes due to primary ageing are more universal and largely unavoidable, those due to secondary ageing do not affect all persons, and are often amenable to interventions and in many cases also to prevention. There are also some grey areas in between primary and secondary ageing: for example, when does the wear and tear on joints and cartilage (primary ageing) become arthritis (secondary ageing)? Unfortunately, with increased age our ability to bounce back from illness or other forms of physical or emotional strain declines. Thus preventative strategies in later life are important, and have as their goal maintaining health and functional capacity for longer before declines occur.

However, the distinction between primary and secondary ageing is important because it focuses attention on elements of the ageing process most amenable to intervention, including self-initiated modifications of lifestyle and health choices. Also, confusion between whether observed changes in an individual are the result of primary or secondary ageing can have negative consequences with respect to healthcare. For individuals to believe that all illness in later life is unavoidable is to miss the opportunity to take proactive steps to improve health and well-being. If a person believes that heart disease or poor balance is an outcome of ageing that must simply be accepted, they will miss the opportunity to change health behaviours that might increase their years as well as quality of life in later life. For healthcare professionals, mistaking secondary ageing processes for primary ageing processes may result in missed diagnostic and treatment opportunities, leading to suboptimal outcomes. If a primary care physician believes depression is a normal part of ageing, he or she may not pursue the variety of empirically validated treatment options available to treat depression in that individual. Untreated secondary ageing may not only lead to poor quality of life, but may in turn exacerbate the negative impacts of primary ageing processes.

Ageing involves lifelong dynamic changes in biological, psychological, and social functioning. These dynamic processes also lead to increasing heterogeneity with increasing age. As Seneca the Younger (4 BCE–65 CE) observed, 'There is not one type of old age for all people.' Why then is it that the older we get, the more different we become from one another?

When we are younger, we have not had much time to experience different circumstances, including life events, lifestyle choices, and our own development and ageing. Over time, people make a variety of choices: they may choose to pursue higher education, have a family, and/or travel; they may smoke, take up exercise, and/or become vegetarian; they may experience medical illness or trauma, be richly rewarded in their career, and/or experience heartache and loss. Over a lifetime the accumulated positive, negative, or mixed experiences and choices, life events, as well as the distinctive biological makeup of each person contribute to this ever-increasing heterogeneity between individuals. This heterogeneity later in life is one of the most interesting aspects of ageing, but one which makes it difficult to untangle what are true primary ageing effects, and how and to what degree changes observed are influenced by this rich interplay of biology, life circumstances, and individual life choices.

Despite difficulties in studying ageing, many theories to account for primary ageing effects have been put forward. These biological theories of ageing have received varying levels of support through experimentation, increasing understanding of the biological bases of maturation, particularly genetics and epigenetics. Innovations in the tools used to study biological functioning and ageing, particularly neuroimaging techniques and molecular biology, have also greatly advanced the field.

Biological theories of ageing

Theories of ageing may be divided roughly into two categories: error theories and programme theories.

Error theories postulate that ageing and death are the result of environmental damage to the body over time. There are many error theories of ageing, including the wear and tear theory, free radical theory, and the somatic DNA damage theory.

The so-called 'wear and tear' theory of ageing points to wear and tear on the organism as the primary driver of ageing at all levels, including the cellular and the molecular. The environment itself can provoke ageing through exposure of the organism to radiation, toxins, and ultraviolet light, all of which can damage both cellular and genetic structures.

The free radical theory of ageing suggests that accumulation of free radicals (unstable oxygen molecules) in the body leads to damage on a cellular level, which drives ageing. Physical processes, such as metabolism of oxygen, produce free radicals, which cause damage to tissue and cells in the body, which can be partially off-set by production of natural anti-oxidants (e.g. certain enzymes) or consumption of foods which are rich in anti-oxidants (such as blueberries and artichokes).

The DNA in our cells is copied when cells divide; over the lifespan errors may creep into this process, leading to genetic mutations. Although the body can correct or eliminate most such mutations, the accumulation of such mutations causes cells to deteriorate and malfunction. Mitochondria, the part of the cell in which energy production occurs, are particularly susceptible to such mutations. This theory of somatic DNA damage focuses only on damage to the genetic integrity of the organism after conception.

The genetic theories posited in *programmed theories of ageing* focus on the genes within sperm and egg cells, thus of the genetic material as it is originally programmed, rather than genetic material altered due to errors or wear and tear. Programme theories of ageing postulate that growth and development in the organism, throughout life, is genetically programmed to follow a pre-determined timeline. Ageing in this set of theories is viewed as an inherent process within the organism rather than simply a result of disease or environmental factors. Ageing and death are a necessary and natural part of the life course, built into the individual's genetic programming. Broad evidence in support of programme theories of ageing includes the fact that within species there is not a lot of variation in lifespan, which tends to be relatively constant.

There are three main theories under the category of programmed ageing theories, each of which poses a different biological system or mechanism as primarily responsible for the ageing process: endocrine theory, immunological theory, and genetic theory (programmed longevity).

Endocrine theories of ageing suggest that decreased production of hormones in later life drives the ageing process. Hormones are a group of molecules that act as chemical messengers in the body. Neurotransmitters are their rough equivalent in the brain, and production of both neurotransmitters and hormones declines with age. Produced in glands such as the thyroid and pituitary glands, hormones regulate such processes and behaviours as metabolism, sleep, and appetite. Wrinkled skin, loss of bone mass and muscle fibre, menopause, and changes to the sleep cycle are primary ageing changes that reflect endocrine system changes in later life. Increasing dysfunction in the endocrine system later in life is linked to diseases such as type II diabetes.

The *immune system theory of ageing* proposes that a less well-functioning immune system drives the ageing process.

In fact, the thymus (which produces many immune cells and is an important part of the immune system) begins to shrink even before age 20, and the functioning of the immune system as a whole peaks in adolescence. Reduced immune system efficiency contributes to the increased incidence of various chronic diseases, many of which have an inflammatory component. Increasing dysfunction in the immune system later in life is linked by some to a range of diseases such as cardiovascular disease, cancer, and Alzheimer's disease.

Programmed longevity posits that ageing results from the sequential switching on and off of certain genes, with a cumulative effect leading to ageing and death. Many aspects of genes seem to play a role in ageing. For example, telomeres, which form the ends of our chromosomes, help to prevent them from fraying, a bit like the plastic ends of shoelaces, and also prevent fusion with other chromosomes. Telomeres gradually become shorter as the cell containing the genetic material divides. When the telomere becomes too short, the cell can no longer divide and it becomes inactive or dies. Research on telomeres and their role in cell division and inactivity (or 'senescence') is the focus in both the cancer and ageing fields.

There is a thought-provoking speculation involving programmed longevity and genetic mutations, namely that some proportion of the population has a genetic make-up that allows individuals to, in effect, postpone ageing. *Genetic instability*, reflected in genes that are more susceptible to mutations, is a precipitating factor for both ageing and certain cancers. Furthermore, there is relatively little chromosomal variation in those over age 80 (the oldest old). These data lead to the hypothesis that perhaps a proportion of the human population has more stable genes, leading such individuals to wear the passage of time lightly. This is also supported by the finding by Evert and colleagues (2003) that, in centenarians, approximately 40 per cent of those who reach age 100 experience diseases of old age at the usual time, around age 65 for most (survivors); while roughly 40 per cent have this experience of chronic age-related diseases pushed back to a later age, roughly age 80 (delayers); with the remaining 20 per cent experiencing minimal or only mild manifestations of chronic age-related diseases (escapers).

Other processes have been studied which appear to affect the ageing process. *Caloric restriction* in animals has been shown to increase lifespan, sometimes dramatically (up to 50 per cent increases in longevity in rats), as well as delay or prevent many age-related diseases. But the caloric restrictions imposed on animals in research settings (typically 30–40 per cent less than the animal would normally consume) have limitations when applied to humans. Moreover, the evidence for similar levels of physiological effects in humans is weak at present. However, the health benefits of the consumption of fewer calories to maintain a healthy weight have wide support, and the potential health benefits of limiting caloric intake for periods during the day or week are the subject of several empirical studies with some promising data emerging.

Epigenetics is a field of growing interest to scientists studying ageing and mortality. Cellular and physiological phenotypic (observable or characteristic) trait variations caused by external or environmental factors that switch genes on and off, as well as affect how cells read genes, are the focus of the field of epigenetics. Such externally or environmentally driven changes, rather than changes in the actual DNA sequence itself—the word epigenetics literally means processes imposed 'on top of' genetic processes—have implications for ageing and age-related changes. New genes are being identified which increase lifespan when mutated or overexpressed—these are known as *gerontogenes*, and epigenetic mechanisms may influence longevity. Increases in variations among epigenetic markers across different cells within the same tissue with increasing age offers evidence that epigenetic alterations may be fundamental to ageing.

The ageing brain

What are the changes that occur in the brain with increasing age? Although a complete discussion of cellular and molecular level brain changes is beyond the scope of this text, important changes in the brain with increasing age include changes to neurotransmitter systems, to connections between brain areas (known as white matter), and to the actual structure, or cytoarchitecture, of discrete brain regions.

With respect to neurotransmitters, with increasing age the production of these molecules, which enable cells to communicate with each other, begins to slow down. Simultaneously, the receptor cells for neurotransmitters also decline in their sensitivity. For example, a neurotransmitter associated with memory, acetylcholine, becomes less abundant with age, and brain receptors associated with acetylcholine also decline in sensitivity. In dementia in general and Alzheimer's disease specifically, acetylcholine levels drop far more precipitously than with normal ageing, as a result of the disease process involved. The ability of certain drugs to increase the amount of acetylcholine in the brain by preventing its recycling or reuptake by the brain is one strategy used to combat decreasing memory abilities associated with this illness.

Neurotransmitters also have a role to play in emotional expression and feeling. Neurotransmitters such as dopamine and serotonin decrease with age, as described earlier with acetylcholine. Researchers have speculated that decreasing serotonin levels may be part of why older adults seem slower to anger than younger persons. This may also underlie why older persons with psychiatric disorders such as schizophrenia, where excessive dopamine is a factor, experience fewer of the more florid symptoms of this disorder, such as hallucinations and delusions, than do younger sufferers.

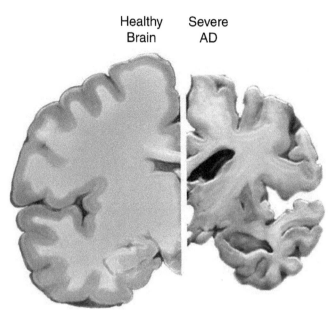

Healthy
Brain

Severe
AD

2. **Healthy brain versus brain with Alzheimer's disease.**

White matter consists of glial cells and myelinated axons which
transmit signals between brain regions. Changes to white matter
fibres are a common feature of increasing age. Most individuals
experience changes in white matter as a consequence of minor
vascular events, many if not most of which go unnoticed by the
individual. In illnesses such as dementia, changes in
white matter connections throughout the brain are much more
profound, and over time, disrupt functionality to the extent that
everyday activities may become difficult or impossible.

In general with increasing age the brain as a whole becomes
smaller, but this is due more to the shrinking volume of brain
cells than to decreases in the number of neurons themselves.

Particular regions of the brain seem more vulnerable to ageing than others. For example, the hippocampus, which plays a central role in memory storage, decreases in size with normal ageing, and is particularly vulnerable to the effects of stress and the production of *cortisol*, the stress hormone. The hippocampus also experiences dramatic and abnormal changes in size and functionality in the face of dementia. As the brain scan in Figure 2 illustrates, there may be substantial structural changes in the brains of older persons experiencing an illness such as dementia compared to those who are healthy.

Brain changes with increasing age have been particularly documented in the areas of the cortex responsible for visual and verbal memory, immediate memory, and the ability to name objects. Non-verbal memory impairments and declines in visuospatial abilities are also considered common cognitive deficits associated with ageing. Age-related changes in the brain, such as decreased temporal lobe volumes, if present, can particularly affect memory.

Changes to the frontal lobes are also common in later life and have an impact on 'executive abilities', a catch-all term for a wide range of planning, emotional regulation, and goal directed activity skills associated with this area of the brain. Executive functions roughly fall into the categories of *organization* and *regulation*. Examples of organization include the ability to sustain attention and to switch focus as required, and to plan and organize tasks; examples of regulation include controlling behaviour and emotions. Mild declines in executive functioning may lead to disorganized thinking and behaviour; more severe disruptions in these abilities, including emotional disregulation, impulsivity, and disinhibition, are more associated with neurological illnesses, such as dementia; and psychiatric illnesses, such as schizophrenia. These age-related functional brain changes may vary considerably between individuals, depending on their education, occupation, hobbies, and skill sets.

Denise Park and Patricia Reuter-Lorenz have put forward their 'Scaffolding Theory of Aging and Cognition-revised' (STAC-r), based on a combination of cognitive data with data from neuroimaging studies to provide an integrated view of how compensatory and adverse neural processes produce varying levels of cognitive functioning in older individuals. A key element of this theory is the idea of *scaffolding*. The older individual compensates for decrements in cognitive functioning by recruiting, in essence, additional brain power from more intact portions of the brain, ones less affected by the ageing process. For example, older adults routinely use both sides of their brain to complete tasks for which younger adults use only one hemisphere. This harnessing of additional cognitive functioning coupled with experience contributes to the finding that older adults often show superior performance on problems requiring complex, relativistic thinking, particularly those demanding recognition of diverse perspectives or the synthesis of contradictory information. STAC-r shows the brain to be a dynamic organ that can adapt to changes in its functioning as a result of the ageing process.

Dementia

Many people mistakenly believe that syndromes such as dementia are to be expected as one grows old. The difference between the memory lapses associated with normal ageing and the significant memory impairments seen for example in Alzheimer's disease are often not clearly understood. However, while decreases in memory functioning and general slowing in processing as well as motor speed are expected parts of normal ageing, the changes associated with dementia go far beyond these, impacting on everyday functioning in a significant way.

Dementia does not affect all adults or even a majority of older adults. For persons over age 65, in most developed and developing countries, approximately 6–8 per cent of individuals will have some form of dementia. For individuals over 80, approximately

20–25 per cent will have some form of dementia. Women are at greater risk of developing dementia, and this is particularly true in very advanced old age, but how much this is due to women's longer lifespan is a matter of debate in the literature. However, in all cases, dementia is not a part of normal or primary ageing but represents a neurological disease process (secondary ageing) characterized by distinct changes in the brain.

A simple definition of dementia would be that it is a change in cognition and/or behaviour that represents a change from prior levels of functioning, such that the individual's daily activities and functioning are negatively and significantly impacted. It is important to note that there must be a change from prior functioning, and this is partly why it is difficult to ascertain the onset of dementia in those with pre-existing developmental difficulties. It also means that care must be taken in not mistaking chronic low levels of intellectual functioning due to other causes (such as head injury or chronic substance abuse) for dementia. The degree of cognitive impairment must be severe enough to impact significantly on functioning to qualify for a diagnosis of dementia, but again for individuals with high premorbid levels of functioning, such changes may be difficult for others to observe and may even be difficult to pick up with neuropsychological testing, as even with some decrements the person may well still be performing at above average levels for his or her age group.

Specific cognitive areas of deficit in dementia often include verbal memory, working (or immediate) memory, spatial memory, language, and executive functioning. It may be difficult for an older person to know when they should be concerned about their cognitive skills. This is especially true in recent times, when greater knowledge of the symptoms of dementia has led to both increased awareness of when to seek help, along with heightened fears over perceived changes in thinking in later life.

In truth it may be very difficult to determine whether changes observed by the individual, those they know, and even health professionals warrant further investigation. If changes persist over time or are quite acute (suggesting some acute causative event such as a stroke), then consultation with a health professional is warranted. If changes in thinking, emotions, or behaviours begin to impact daily life and particularly familiar tasks, such as way-finding (i.e. getting lost in familiar places), then seeking professional advice is probably warranted.

When people think of dementia, they often think primarily about changes to cognition and thinking. But many non-cognitive symptoms and behaviours may also signal the potential presence of dementia. Odd or inappropriate behaviours, repeated falls or loss of balance, changes in eating behaviours and dietary preferences (for example, a shift to a marked preference for sweets can be associated with some forms of dementia), neglecting hygiene, and an increase in apathy all can signal a progressive neurological condition. In such cases it is important to rule out cognitive or behavioural changes due to worry or depression; physiological changes, such as metabolic disorders or neoplastic (cancerous) diseases; or medication side effects.

There are many forms of dementia, with distinct causes and symptom profiles. Alzheimer's disease is the most common form of dementia (estimated at 50–70 per cent of cases) and its onset in individuals is generally after the age of 65. Vascular dementia is caused by cerebrovascular disease with or without acute events such as strokes. Vascular dementia is relatively rare on its own and most commonly co-occurs with Alzheimer's disease. Frontotemporal dementias generally encompass a range of disorders characterized by changes in the frontotemporal portions of the brain, with changes in behaviours, higher order judgement and planning skills, and/or language as prominent features. Dementia with Lewy Bodies is characterized by progressive declines in cognition in addition to such symptoms as waxing and waning attention, recurring visual hallucinations, and changes in motor movements that resemble Parkinson's disease. This latter symptom is due to the fact that Lewy Bodies, which are a feature of Parkinson's disease in subcortical brain regions, appear in cortical brain regions in dementia with Lewy Bodies.

The mean duration for the most common forms of dementia, such as Alzheimer's disease, from diagnosis to death, is around 7–10 years, although the range can be as great as 3–20 years. Earlier diagnosis currently means that individuals have a greater chance of living longer with dementia, but also with a better chance to access treatments and services at an earlier point, enabling them to make crucial decisions themselves about such things as financial arrangements and care. In instances of persons showing symptoms of dementia at a younger age or having highly genetically determined forms of the disease, the latter generally progresses at a more rapid rate. Age itself remains the greatest single risk factor for the development of dementia. Since currently disease modifying treatments are lacking (i.e. further neurophysiological declines cannot be slowed by current medical treatments), the mean duration period noted earlier basically corresponds to a rough estimate of survival until death.

There are many factors that increase risk for dementia; as mentioned, increasing age is the primary (and most unavoidable) risk factor. In Alzheimer's disease, about 70 per cent of the risk of getting the disease is believed to be genetic, with a number of genes involved in the various subtypes of this illness. Life events such as head injury may increase risk of developing dementia. There are many lifestyle factors such as smoking, inactivity, and obesity that increase the risk of dementia. Low levels of mental stimulation or social interaction also put one at risk for dementia; brain regions that are inactive experience shrinkage and may open the door to increased cognitive decline. Diet may play a role, and diets that increase risk for vascular events generally also increase risk for dementia. Some foods, such as those that contain anti-oxidants (e.g. blueberries) or omega-three fatty acids (e.g. salmon) may have some protective benefits against age-related changes in physical or mental well-being. The potential health benefits of the Mediterranean diet (which emphasizes eating primarily plant-based foods, replacing butter with olive oil, and using spices and herbs instead of salt to add flavour) have also been the subject of promising research. Exercise and physical activity, as well as minimizing times of inactivity such as sitting, are also important for general health as well as cognitive and emotional well-being, and certainly contribute to lowering the risk of dementia.

Many studies have replicated the finding that higher levels of education are associated with lower risk of developing dementia. Several hypotheses have been advanced to explain this finding, and indeed the finding itself probably is driven by more than one factor. For example, cognitive reserve refers to the idea that people with greater complexity in their neural networks, for example due to higher levels of education or holding a stimulating occupation, may help stave off the effects of cognitive decline due to a greater degree of reserve available to be drawn upon. In essence, such people can afford to lose some brain cells and connections as they have more in reserve. In the case of dementia, for example, the effects of the disease may take longer to manifest in such individuals with a robust cognitive reserve. The study of seasoned taxi drivers in London, whose hippocampi were greatly enlarged after memorization of complex routes in that city, would offer confirmatory evidence of the cognitive reserve hypothesis (as well as potentially offering an intriguing occupational route to decreased risk of dementia).

Although most research in dementia has been carried out in Western developed countries, the 10/66 Dementia Research Group has set out to change this state of affairs. These researchers carry out population-based research into dementia, non-communicable diseases, and ageing in middle and low income countries. The moniker '10/66' indicates the fact that only 10 per cent or less of total population-based research has been carried out in the developing world, and yet this is where 66 per cent of the world's dementia sufferers live. The 10/66 group is part of Alzheimer's Disease International (ADI), an international federation of Alzheimers associations throughout the world, which is also associated with the World Health Organization.

ADI publishes a world Alzheimer report each year. In 2010, the ADI reported how the burden of dementia would disproportionately affect developing countries going forward, based on these countries' ageing populations. They forecast a 40 per cent increase in numbers of persons with dementia in Europe; 63 per cent in North America; 77 per cent in the southern Latin American countries; and 89 per cent in developed Asia Pacific countries. However, in less developed regions of the world the figures were much higher, including 117 per cent growth in persons with dementia in East Asia; 107 per cent in South Asia, 134–46 per cent in the rest of Latin America; and 125 per cent in north Africa and the Middle East.

Currently there is no cure for most causes of dementia. Pharmacological approaches can assist some persons with dementia to experience reduced cognitive and functional effects of their disease, thus allowing for greater time spent living independently in the community. Similarly, psychosocial approaches to support the person with dementia can prove valuable. Such approaches range from strategies for improving memory to support groups to share losses as well as coping strategies and individual counselling to assist the person with dementia to put their affairs in order and possibly to address interpersonal ruptures that they wish to mend. Also, organizations such as the various Alzheimers associations worldwide offer advice and support in negotiating such tasks as appointing a trusted person as a financial guardian and guidance in planning for nursing-home admission.

Caregivers of persons with dementia are vulnerable to both physical and mental health issues as a result of caring for a person with dementia. Caregiving is an overwhelmingly female occupation, and overall the largest proportion of caregivers of persons with dementia is composed of spouses who themselves are often of advanced age. Levels of psychological distress and stress are significantly higher, and subjective well-being and physical health significantly lower, in caregivers of persons with dementia compared to other caregivers. Studies also suggest that if the person with dementia is depressed, then the caregiver has a greatly increased chance of becoming depressed themselves. Importantly, interventions aimed at improving caregiver well-being may delay nursing-home placement for the care recipient, in some studies by an average time of 1.5 years as compared to placement for care recipients whose caregiver received no such intervention.

Much research has documented the specific ways in which caregiving impacts caregivers. This ranges from negative impacts on the immune system through to depression and increased morbidity and mortality. However, caregivers themselves report positive aspects of caregiving, and recent research has sought a more balanced and nuanced view of caregiving. For example, the prior relationship between the caregiver and care recipient greatly affects the nature of the caregiving relationship, for good or ill. Caregivers of various religious denominations may expect greater or lesser support based on what their faith sees as the roles of caregiver, church, and community. Caregivers report that some respite from caregiving offers some of the greatest relief from the burden of caregiving. A variety of psychosocial interventions, including cognitive behavioural therapy and acceptance and commitment therapy, whether individual or group-based, have been shown to be effective in reducing caregiver burden and improving well-being.

The ageing body

It is well-established that physical health and physical functioning decline over the life course, particularly in later life (after age 60 or 65). A rise in chronic disease and other conditions such as arthritis, high blood pressure and obesity can cause loss in function and lead to generally decreasing trajectories for health over the lifespan. Self-reported physical symptoms reflecting both primary and secondary ageing changes on average increase linearly with increasing age. Declines in physical functioning and increased disability have important implications for the ability to live independently and experience good quality of life in one's later years. Declines in health are linked to adverse events such as increased risk of falls, increased use of healthcare services, and increased likelihood of admission to nursing-home care. Increasingly, *multimorbidity* (having multiple chronic conditions) has an adverse impact on quality of life and increases the complexity of disease management in older patients; in the developed world more than half of older adults have three or more chronic conditions.

Organ and sensory systems change in predictable ways in response to primary ageing. However, it is important to note that such ageing changes become apparent often in mid-life (if not earlier), whereas a handful of changes are only experienced at the very end of life. For example, maximal lung capacity declines beginning in young adulthood and continues to decline until age 70. Difficulty seeing objects in close detail may start at around age 40; hearing by contrast declines later in life, and particularly for higher pitched sounds. Decreases in sensory or organ functioning can not only decrease the ability to perform day-to-day tasks, but may impact negatively on the ability to maintain social connections and positive well-being. For example, hearing loss may cause retreat from group social activities, and lead to increased social isolation and depression. Difficulty with perception and motor functioning may likewise impair driving ability, which in turn may negatively impact mobility, social connections, and sense of independence. Changes in sensory, perception, motor, and vestibular functioning can lead to decreased brain stimulation and may precipitate cognitive declines. Thus it is important that any potentially modifiable changes in these systems are recognized and treated early.

There are many cardiovascular system changes with ageing, notably stiffening of arteries, increasing the load on the heart to keep blood circulating. Both the kidneys and the liver become less efficient at clearing waste from the body. Bones begin to lose their density by age 35, and muscle tone declines about 20 per cent by age 70. Some of these changes can be partially modified through diet and exercise, although many cannot and must be adapted to or compensated for with assistive devices (such as reading glasses or hearing aids). Some changes are subtle yet may have more profound effects on health. For example, the perception of thirst decreases after age 85, such that over 40 per cent of persons in this age range are insufficiently hydrated, which can in turn affect other organ systems as well as cognitive functioning.

Age-related illness in later life, particularly chronic disease, may lead to decreased functioning and quality of life. In order to assist both research and interventions in this area, a quantification of the so-called *burden of disease* experienced by individuals has been developed, using a metric called the disability-adjusted-life-year (DALY). The DALY metric (see Figure 3) combines years of life lost due to premature mortality and years of life lost due to the amount of time lived in states of less than full health. Such burden of disease estimates have been useful for researchers as well as organizations such as the WHO, who track and compare burden of disease and DALYs globally.

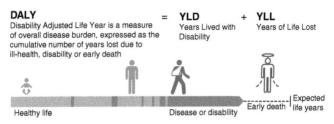

DALY = **YLD** + **YLL**
Disability Adjusted Life Year is a measure of overall disease burden, expressed as the cumulative number of years lost due to ill-health, disability or early death | Years Lived with Disability | Years of Life Lost

Healthy life | Disease or disability | Early death | Expected life years

3. **Disability adjusted life years.**

Frailty can be conceptualized as the intersection between chronic disease states, decreased functioning, and increasing vulnerability to further declines in health. Although a single agreed upon definition for frailty remains elusive, frailty in later life is usually understood to include low physical activity, muscle weakness, slowed performance (both in movement and in thinking), fatigue or poor endurance, and unintentional weight loss. It is increasingly the subject of study as those older adults in this clinical state have greatly increased vulnerability to physical illness, as well as decreased ability to cope with adverse life events (e.g. falls) or other stressors. Most frail older adults are over age 80 and often require assistance in their activities of daily living, such as eating, dressing, and mobility. Risk factors for becoming frail in later life include smoking, a history of depression, chronic medical conditions over many years, and being underweight for their height and age. Frailty affects roughly 25 per cent of those over age 85. With the number of individuals over 80 increasing rapidly as a proportion of the population in most countries, and with the many negative health outcomes as well as increased cost of care to individuals who become frail, research identifying at-risk individuals as well as exploring preventative strategies is important.

Disease trajectories later in life

Historically, death often overtook the individual swiftly. People died from acute illnesses which developed over days or weeks and quickly led to death. Many deaths were the result of accidents or trauma, again with only a short time from onset to death. With public health, safety and medical advances, sudden death is more uncommon now than in prior centuries. But chronic disease or adverse events such as a broken hip can adversely affect disability and disease trajectories in old age. Later in life people currently develop one or more chronic diseases, with often insidious onset and only gradual worsening of symptoms and declines in functioning. Three distinct trajectories for persons with chronic illness later in life have been described. The first is a trajectory for most cancers, namely a steady progression but often only mild decline until a clear terminal stage is reached; a trajectory of steeper decline with intermittent periods of rapid decline and some recovery, ending in a more sudden precipitous decline to death, reflecting illnesses such as heart or lung failure; and the prolonged gradual decline typical of persons who are frail or who have dementia.

Often individuals report that ideally they would like to die in their sleep, and a common fear at the end of life is to die alone. Palliative care regimes have made great strides in recent years in providing terminally ill patients with a pain-free and dignified death. Knowing the various trajectories of decline associated with specific illnesses can better equip both family and friends as well as health professionals to help the individual manage their illness, providing care and assistance that reflects the individual's trajectory while considering their own wishes and context.

Biological ageing is challenging to study, because the effects of primary ageing are often diffuse, affecting different systems at different rates, and also the process of ageing affects individuals differently. Part of a person's individual responses to the ageing process is linked to biological processes such as genetics and the individual's propensity to develop specific illnesses (e.g. cardiovascular disease). Some variations have to do with lifestyle choices, such as exercise, smoking, and dietary intake. Finally, one's gender, educational attainment, early developmental history, and socioeconomic status influence responses to biological ageing. Of course, all of these factors may also influence brain functioning, as well as the more psychological and interpersonal aspects of ageing. In Chapter 3, we will turn our attention to psychological aspects of ageing.

Chapter 3
The psychology of ageing

One generation plants the trees, another gets the shade.

(Chinese proverb)

Psychological aspects of ageing are some of the most intriguing in the science of gerontology. Psychological theories of ageing encompass mental health and emotional well-being as well as changes in these states, at both individual and interpersonal levels, associated with increasing age. Cognitive aspects of ageing, including changes in thinking and behaviour as a result of both primary and secondary ageing, will be reviewed here, as well as how personality and emotions are expressed in later life.

Ways of studying changes in functioning over time

One way of studying ageing is to compare different persons at various ages on their performance on a specific task or some aspect of functioning. But the drawback to this approach is that it introduces potential biases in interpreting any data obtained. An everyday example would be if we tested older and younger persons on how well they could use an iPad. We might conclude that older persons are not as good at using new technology (a common conclusion). However, this would be erroneous; the younger group is likely to have had far more experience in using the iPad than the older group. If we compared older persons and younger persons with the same degree of familiarity with iPads, then this (at least in part) would address the concern that a difference ascribed to *ageing* was really reflecting a difference in *experience*.

In another example, if persons of different ages were compared on a test of general intelligence, it would be tempting to ascribe the differences in their performance to their age. But *cohort effects* may be at play. 'Cohort effects' describe the similarities of a group of individuals who have developed and experienced a similar set of circumstances over time. For example, the schooling system for particular birth cohorts may vary dramatically, and may contribute to how individuals at different ages perform on a specific set of tasks, such as arithmetic problems. Or persons living through particular epochs in history may experience significant events (the Great Depression; the Global Financial Crisis) and these individuals may then develop different attitudes to financial risk when compared with those who in their formative years did not experience such economic hardship. Individuals in these different birth cohorts may answer questions about their willingness to take risks with their money in different ways due to their experiences—to interpret their different responses solely in terms of their age differences would be both misleading and incorrect.

In terms of disentangling cohort effects, both *cross-sectional* study designs, where different cohorts of individuals are compared at only one point in time, and *longitudinal* study designs, where a single cohort is followed across time, have significant limitations. The *sequential* study design, where the different birth cohorts are recruited and followed over time, allows for better control of cohort effects. Early cross-sectional studies of intelligence in the 1930s and 1940s showed intelligence as declining in later years. Later longitudinal studies of intelligence show much less individual variation across time and with increasing age than the cross-sectional studies had demonstrated. Sequential studies allowed further comparisons of how various cognitive skills change both over time and between generations. Longitudinal studies, particularly of ageing cohorts, often have their own biases such that healthier individuals with higher general socioeconomic status and educational levels tend to remain in the study longer, compared to individuals lacking such advantages; this effect is largely mitigated in sequential designs.

Longitudinal and sequential studies of ageing are important in exploring connections between our internal states and external circumstances in later life. Such data is important in informing not only empirical conceptualizations of the ageing process, but also public policy. For example, the Australian Longitudinal Study of Women's Health (ALSWH) has for many years helped shape government and health service policy and practice in Australia, with its collection of data from young, middle-aged, and older samples over many decades. In 2011, the study published findings from a collaborative research effort with the longitudinal Perth Men's study, examining whether the Australian National Health Guidelines were in line with actual data from older individuals over time. The findings indicated that some modifications in the guidelines for older persons would better match actual health outcomes data. For example, the general Body Mass Index (BMI) guidelines were found to be overly restrictive when applied to older persons, in that slightly higher than recommended BMI levels appeared protective (rather than a risk) for health in older individuals. The research results also emphasized the benefits of quitting smoking, even at advanced ages.

Such data are invaluable, but also must be on-going, as successive waves of individuals moving through time bring with them their own unique cohort attributes, which in turn affect their internal and external responses on various health, psychological, and social measures and indicators of well-being and functioning.

Psychological theories of ageing

Psychological theories of ageing have advanced our understanding of the active and dynamic aspects of ageing, and for the most part have emphasized older adults' active role in managing their own ageing process. This accords with advice from ancient thinkers such as Galen (129-200 CE), urging their peers to actively take care of themselves so as to age as well as possible. However, the earliest modern theory of later life, of ageing as a passive process largely beyond the control of the individual, harks back to authors such as Horace (Roman, 65-8 BCE) who viewed many aspects of ageing as negative and inevitable. (Of course, death is unquestionably the most inevitable aspect of ageing, despite our best attempts at avoidance (Figure 4.))

The *disengagement theory of ageing*, one of the first theories of ageing proposed by modern gerontologists, held that older adults need to withdraw from society as they age, and that this is of benefit to the older individual as well as society: the older

"Getting warm...warmer."

4. Death, in the end, comes for us all...

individual will not become overwhelmed, and younger members of society can surge forward. In contrast, the *activity theory of ageing*, formulated in response to the disengagement theory of ageing, proposed that remaining active and socially engaged contributes to successful ageing. The *continuity theory of ageing*, which posits that older adults usually maintain the same activities and interaction patterns in later life as they did earlier in life, attempting to maintain this activity by adapting strategies connected to their past experiences and circumstances, is a later elaboration upon the activity theory of ageing.

How we might best adapt to the ageing process is the focus of Paul Baltes's 'Selection, Optimization and Compensation Theory of Successful Aging' (SOC). This theory suggests that individuals who age successfully actively use three strategies to make this transition into later life possible: selection, optimization, and compensation. Selection includes identifying relevant goals, prioritizing them, and recognizing when they have been achieved. Optimization refers to the use of strategies to facilitate successful achievement of set goals. Compensation refers to the individual adapting to limitations (perhaps due to ageing processes) that interfere with achieving their goal, including the use of devices (as simple as reading glasses or as complex as a smartphone).

The classic example of an individual successfully using such strategies is the pianist Arthur Rubinstein (1887–1982), who continued to pursue a concert career well into his 80s. Rubinstein did this by playing a smaller selection of pieces (selection), practising these pieces more often (optimization), and using larger tempo contrasts in his playing to (compensate) for the fact that he could not play as fast as he once had. These small changes of tempo were largely not evident to audiences, allowing the pianist to continue pursuing what he loved to do. The SOC theory demonstrates how thoughtful approaches to selection of goals and active compensatory strategies may improve well-being in later life.

Older adults need good strategies to continue to adapt to their own ageing, at a time when resources (physical, financial, and so forth) might be in short supply. One resource that was thought to be in short supply for many older persons was social support; in many surveys older persons reported fewer social contacts with increasing age. However, when researchers looked into older adults' *perceived social support*, they found that older individuals reported equal, if not greater, levels of social support than younger age groups, even though they had fewer individuals in their social network. Why might this be? How might the way older adults view and use their social networks be different to younger persons?

Laura Carstensen was one researcher very intrigued by this finding. Her 'Socioemotional Selectivity Theory' evolved as she sought to understand how growing older shifts the way people view their friendship networks. The key lies in perception of time—as we age, we essentially recognize that we have lived more of our lives than we have left to live, and this leads us to prioritize those relationships from which the greatest meaning and satisfaction are derived.

However, shrinking social networks are again not a passive activity—older adults actively prune their social networks so that they are able to focus on their most important and cherished relationships. This is different to persons at other points in their life. For younger people, having a large social network is valuable, as early in life one is finding one's place in the world, and settling into new roles (e.g. being a parent) as well as making decisions (e.g. should I study further or find work?). In the middle years many people have by and large settled on a pattern of activities and so a smaller group of friends with similar interests proves more useful (e.g. parents groups; work colleagues). These fewer but more intense relationships can assist in providing support and more targeted information. Finally, in later life, older adults actively disengage from persons who provide only minimal social support, or who are more of a drain on the older adult's resources.

Social support itself has been the focus of research, and Toni Antonucci's 'Convoy Theory' highlights three key benefits of social support. These include aid (or instrumental support), which includes such things as helping out with tasks; and affect (or emotional support), which would include providing emotional support. Many surveys find that not having persons with whom you can confide, who will be supportive in times of strife, is a risk factor for poor physical and emotional health. Finally, Antonucci states that affirmation, which reflects the intangible communication between members of a social network, including shared values, goals, and aspirations, is also an important function of social support. However, it is also important to remember that poor interpersonal relationships may have a negative impact on health and well-being, and some research suggests that the harmful effects of bad relationships may exceed the positive benefits of good relationships—an important consideration in later life when fewer coping resources may be available than earlier in life.

Antonucci's idea of affirmation leads naturally to a discussion of the benefits of groups of friends or more formal group membership, be it a bird watching club, a political party, or one's nationality. *Social identity theory* has been put forward as a way of looking at how group membership affects behaviour and even how you think about yourself. The theory holds that one's identity develops in part through interactions with groups, and expectations that develop through membership of the group can influence behaviour. For example, older adults are more likely to think that they require a hearing aid if they are encouraged to think of themselves as belonging to the group, 'elderly people'. In another study, receiving larger amounts

of social support was found to be less important to positive
well-being in older persons than providing support to others.
Receiving support is associated with dependency, while providing
social support is seen as socially productive—a more positive
'identity'.

Social identity theory also has frameworks with which to look
at health, particularly in later life. Group membership has
been linked to improved health and functioning, with levels of
well-being higher amongst those who belonged to the greater
number of groups. Another study, of residents in a nursing home,
found that those residents who were involved as a group in
decisions concerning the decoration of their shared spaces in the
home displayed increased social identification with staff and
fellow residents, and increased life satisfaction. These findings
suggest that potentially the power of group memberships could be
used to improve well-being in later life.

Normal ageing: changes to aspects of cognitive functioning

Although people think of later life as a time when the brain loses
functionality, in actual fact the greatest number of brain cells is
lost before the end of the first year of life. This loss of brain cells
early in life is a type of pruning; the brain has the capacity to learn
and absorb much information, but the areas of the brain and the
types of processes that are most utilized will be retained and
strengthened, while those that are not used will fall away. This is
illustrated most clearly with language acquisition; although all
children are initially able to learn all languages, the ability to form
certain sounds, if not utilized, will be more difficult or impossible
to pick up later in life.

Language is one of the most robust cognitive skills in the face of
ageing, and by and large does not figure in losses associated with

primary ageing. People continue to increase their vocabulary, for example, well into their eighth decade of life. This then makes changes in language of particular concern later in life. Unlike memory, which is subject to changes that are expected in the course of primary ageing, the ability to understand what is said and make a sensible reply (known as receptive and expressive language function, respectively) should remain strong in later life. Changes in either receptive or expressive language function may reflect an acute event such as a stroke in the brain, or a more insidious process such as a developing tumour or other malignancy in the brain, or the onset of a progressive neurological condition such as dementia. With regards to the language abilities associated with normal ageing, the ability to generate specific words (as opposed to speaking and understanding words) declines with age, particularly after age 70, and declines more quickly than the ability to name objects. For example, with increasing age it becomes more difficult to generate lists of words beginning with a certain letter, or words of a certain category, such as items of clothing.

In contrast, motor skills begin to decline in early adulthood, particularly with respect to speed and reaction time. Hand–eye coordination and fine motor skills certainly show declines by midlife, although those who maintain motor skills with high levels of practice over many years, such as athletes or musicians, may well retain their task-specific motor skills into middle age and beyond.

Memory and its decline is perhaps the one cognitive domain most associated with increasing age and primary ageing, and is of increasing concern to people as they age. Improving one's memory is the subject of many self-help books, and the focus of much research in terms of attempts to help healthy individuals maintain their memory abilities, and assist those with declining memory to retain or even perhaps regain as much functioning as possible.

There are many types of memory processes. Short-term memory includes the information we are currently working with or processing (often referred to as 'working memory') as well as information simply held (but not manipulated) for short periods of time (generally up to 30 seconds). Long-term memory involves those memories held and kept available for retrieval at a later date, which include information gleaned over the lifespan. Within long-term memory, memory for events and experiences is known as episodic memory, and memory for facts and concepts is known as semantic memory. Procedural memory includes memory for skills and tasks.

Generally, with increasing age, the greatest declines are seen in episodic memory, with lesser deficits seen in semantic memory. Procedural memory remains relatively robust in the face of both primary and secondary ageing, as even persons with dementia retain many motor skills until quite advanced stages of their disease process. This means that if Mary is taking tennis lessons, her memory for the name of the instructor, and the timing or even actual recall of events that happen during a particular lesson, are more vulnerable to memory deficits associated with primary ageing. But over time, if Mary attends the lessons regularly, her stroke and return should improve. Note that this example works to a certain extent even if the person in question had a disease associated with secondary ageing, such as Alzheimer's disease. In this case, explicit memory might be almost completely disturbed, leading to little recall for any aspect of the tennis lesson, but some improvement in the actual mechanics of the game, which involve procedural memory, may occur over time. This is why driving is such an issue with persons diagnosed with dementia; although many aspects of the task (e.g. responding to road signs; attending to conditions on the road) are impaired, the actual procedural memory for how to start the car and the mechanics of driving the vehicle remain intact. (See Table 3.)

Table 3 Changes due to primary and secondary ageing: psychological/cognitive

Primary ageing changes	Secondary ageing changes
Recall from memory slower	Depression and anxiety
Procedural memory remains relatively intact	Stroke resulting in loss of language ability
Reduced ability to adapt and self-regulate in the face of environmental changes (e.g. in cold or hot weather)	Poor health outcomes due to lifestyle choices (smoking, lack of exercise)
Somewhat reduced reaction time and speed of thinking	Parkinson's disease results in drastic changes in speed of movement and thought
Somewhat slowed speed at which nerve cells conduct information	Dementia may result in dramatic changes in personality

Primary and secondary ageing: effects on cognitive and psychological functioning

One theory of how older adults might cope with memory loss is the idea of 'interactive minds' or 'cognitive collaboration'. This is the situation where an older person discussing a memory or telling a story benefits from interactions with others, whose questions or interjections help jog memory and build a richer response than if the person simply had to rely on their own memory. This might also partially underlie the loss of functioning, including cognitive functioning, which can occur when such close friends, family, and spouses die, or when the older adult must function on their own in institutional settings such as nursing homes.

As was demonstrated in research with longitudinal studies of cognitive changes over the lifespan, there are many areas of brain functioning that remain robust later in life. However, these changes vary between individuals, and even the amount that they vary between individuals may be considerable. For example, the amount of variation between individuals as they age in terms of many aspects of language, such as the ability to name objects, is relatively small. But the amount of variation between motor speed varies much more between individuals as they age—reflecting in part the greater reliance of motor skills on the intactness of the central nervous system.

Variation in rates of change in cognitive skills with increasing age depends upon many factors. As mentioned, repeated practice and honing of certain cognitive skills, whether because of one's occupation (for example, an accountant's facility with numbers) or one's hobby (for example, the word knowledge of a crossword puzzle enthusiast), will tend to make these particular cognitive skills more robust not only in the face of primary ageing but also in the face of disease processes such as dementia. Environmental and psychosocial factors may also play a role in cognitive health; higher levels of intellectual stimulation and education, getting exercise and good sleep, avoiding stress, and engaging in meaningful activities are all predictive of better cognitive health in later life.

There are also many myths about what functional changes may be a consequence of an ageing brain. For example, older drivers in generally good physical and cognitive health drive as well if not better than young adults. The older brain has collected much experience pertinent to safe driving, such as experience of when to scan for potential hazards. Similarly, older adults in generally good physical and cognitive health are unlikely to fall for scams, or at least do so at no greater rate than younger adults. Old age in and of itself is not a risk factor for declines in such functional capacities, but dementia and/or poor health are. Dementia can make such activities unsafe for both the person with dementia and others, and even physical disabilities (such as severe arthritis, limiting mobility including looking in mirrors) can render driving unsafe for such individuals.

Research has demonstrated the remarkable plasticity of the brain even into later life; we now know that new brain cells and neural connections can form, or be eroded, by exposure to stimuli in the environment. The brain's changes do not all lead to functional decrements: for example, the corpus callosum, the dense bridge of connections between the two hemispheres in the brain, changes with age to compensate for gradually decreasing neuronal reserves, with a by-product of enhanced connectivity between the hemispheres, thus better using total brain capacity and potentially augmenting particular problem-solving abilities in later life—as reflected in the STAC-r theory of cognitive ageing discussed in the previous chapter.

Similarly, epidemiological research has illustrated the complex interaction of risk and protective factors on cognition in later life. For example, numerous studies have shown a negative impact on cognitive functioning of smoking and excess body weight, whereas a similarly large and growing body of literature has demonstrated positive effects on physical and mental health in later life of participating in exercise and maintaining social networks. Indeed, there is some evidence that such risk and protective factors for general health and well-being may also have positive and negative effects, to some extent, on the risk of developing dementia in later life.

Primary and secondary ageing: effects on emotional experiences and personality functioning

The effects of age on the experience of emotions and well-being over the lifespan are as varied as its effects on physical and cognitive functioning. Many studies show that people's experiences of positive and negative emotions are for the most part independent phenomena, rather than being two ends of the same spectrum. Furthermore, the experience of positive and negative emotions follows independent trajectories over time. Longitudinal research suggests decreases in the experience of negative emotions from young through middle adulthood, followed by relative stability after age 60. The experience of positive emotions tends to be relatively stable until later in life, when declines are reported in some, but not all, studies; in some studies these declines do not appear until well into one's 70s. However, emotional stability appears to increase linearly with increasing age, such that as we age, we report less in the way of swings in our mood, and less of a tendency to experience extreme emotional states. Research into specific biological mechanisms and pathways to explain these emotional changes in later life is on-going.

Irrespective of the mechanism, many older adults report this growing emotional stability in later life as a positive experience. Well-being encompasses positive emotional health as well as social functioning and engagement in meaningful activities; again, research on well-being over the lifespan suggests a U-shaped curve, with gains in early adulthood and some levelling off in advanced old age. Older adults also appear more comfortable in the face of negative emotions such as sadness, which may contribute to their relatively superior performance in some studies on tasks involving resolution of complex, emotionally charged problems. Greater facility in managing interpersonal conflict is also reported later in life. Finally, older adults are also more likely to experience complex or mixed emotions than younger persons, for example feeling happiness tinged with regret. Researchers have found that older persons keeping a daily diary of emotional experiences report a greater range of emotions than younger adults, as well as experiencing emotions almost completely absent in younger adults' diaries, such as poignant feelings associated with reminiscence.

Overall, older adults appear to have quite complex emotional experiences.

Later life brings changes to personality functioning as well as emotional functioning. Personality traits are generally defined as relatively enduring patterns of thoughts, feelings, and behaviours that make us who we are as individuals. While personality had been thought to be relatively stable in later life, new research demonstrates that personality traits can and do change throughout life, and that such changes can be substantial. For example, both cross-sectional and longitudinal research has shown that older adults tend to score higher on agreeableness and conscientiousness, and lower on extraversion, neuroticism, and openness, than younger individuals. It is important to note that, of course, such studies are reporting on population changes and averages, and that individuals can change to a greater or lesser extent than is represented by such averages. With respect to later life, research demonstrates that older people retain the capacity to change patterns of thoughts, feelings, and behaviours. Findings from centenarian studies suggest that extraversion and a tendency to reach out to others is characteristic of persons who attain this great age.

Personality traits have been associated with both more and less successful ageing outcomes. For instance, possessing the personality trait of conscientiousness, which can include a sense of responsibility, self-control, and traditionalism, has, in several studies, been associated with greater longevity. Higher levels of neuroticism, which can include greater emotional reactivity and the tendency to interpret situations as threatening, is associated with greater risk of experiencing poor physical and mental health. More serious disturbances in personality functioning, known as personality disorders, have a negative effect on mental health and interpersonal functioning throughout the lifespan, including later life. As mentioned previously, abrupt changes in personality may be associated with a range of physical disorders, including strokes and various forms of dementia.

For many people, the stereotype of older adults is of individuals who are rigid and inflexible in their personalities, who are more likely to suffer from illnesses such as depression and anxiety. In fact, one's risk of developing any psychiatric disorder *other than dementia* declines after age 65. For example, instances of anxiety and depression, in their full-blown clinical forms, currently are less prevalent at later ages than at younger ages—recent systematic review studies suggest lower incidence rates of depression and anxiety in later life (although this may represent a cohort effect). Many illnesses (such as schizophrenia) peak in early adulthood, in terms of risk. The reporting of depression and anxiety in later life may change as the Baby Boomer cohort ages, but at the time of writing mental disorders such as depression and anxiety are reported relatively less frequently later in life compared to those at younger ages, and milder forms (or *subthreshold*) expressions of these disorders are also more common for older adults.

Furthermore, symptom expression is different at various ages—for example, depression in younger children is often characterized by changes in patterns of interacting with peers and behavioural disturbances. In older individuals, cognitive changes are often the most significant symptom reported. And this often leads to the older depressed or anxious adult being misdiagnosed with dementia. In one study in the US, upon autopsy, a significant percentage of patients who had been diagnosed with a dementia were found to have been misdiagnosed—and the most common missed diagnosis was depression, upon retrospective chart review.

Why might late-life depression prove to be a tricky diagnosis to make? The typical symptoms of depression reported in mid-life—changes in appetite, changes to sleep, lack of enjoyment in activities, low energy, and feeling sad—may either be misinterpreted in later life or ascribed to normal ageing. Often medications or even illnesses may create many of these symptoms. In addition, people, including health professionals, may operate under a myth that older persons naturally become lonely or disengaged with life as they age. When risk factors for depression (e.g. poor self-perceived health) and anxiety (e.g. a history of childhood physical or sexual abuse) in later life occur in socioeconomically deprived populations, individuals may in turn face the added complication of having the poorest access to mental health services. All of these are powerful barriers to older adults getting properly assessed and treated for any psychiatric symptoms appearing in later life.

Protective factors for mental health are also being researched; for example, in the case of late-life anxiety, high perceived social support and regular exercise have been shown to be protective against the development of anxiety disorders in later life. In general, better physical health is predictive of better emotional as well as cognitive health in later life.

Bereavement is often associated with both depression and later life. Yet older adults take about the same time as other age groups to return to prior levels of functioning following bereavement. Grief and the management of loss, later in life as in earlier points in the lifespan, is an extremely individual process, and may be affected by a person's social and environmental context. The presence of additional risk factors for depression, such as social isolation and functional disability, may increase the chance of developing depression as a reaction to bereavement in later life.

Physical health can also have a direct impact on emotional well-being in older persons. There is an unfortunate negative feedback loop between the experience of depression and poor health throughout the lifespan. In later years this can have an increasingly detrimental effect on the ability to function independently and have a reasonable quality of life. While many chronic illnesses may only be amenable to moderate symptom relief, undiagnosed and/or untreated physical illness leaves the older adult with an *excess burden* to carry. If some form of treatment were received, either to provide relief of physical symptoms or to improve psychological coping, at least some resolution in distress might occur.

Similarly, experiencing stress can have a negative impact on physical, emotional, and social well-being in later life. Much research has focused on negative outcomes to specific life events (such as bereavement) or response to chronic medical conditions or symptoms (such as diabetes or pain). However, there is a small literature exploring some positive outcomes of experiencing moderate levels of stress, such as developing enhanced coping mechanisms and even a possible decrease in risk of illnesses such as dementia. The relationship between stress and physical or emotional well-being is that these relationships work both ways—so that stress can contribute to depression, for example, and being depressed can in turn contribute to one's appraisal of stressful events. The key to understanding stress effects is to recognize that part of what drives the response to stress is the individual's perception of it, and whether they have the resources to cope with the stress and its effects. Potential sources of stress, such as ageism and chronic health problems, are particularly closely associated with later life and may have significant effects on health and emotional well-being. Resilience to stress is an active area of research with older persons and is described in more detail in later chapters.

Treatment of mental disorders in later life

Generational influences can impact older adults in whether they choose to seek help from mental health services—older adults from earlier generations are often perceived as stoic and unwilling to ask for such services. One barrier to seeking mental health services that crosses age and cultural barriers is the sense among some sectors of society of there being a great stigma attached to such services. Another barrier to seeking this sort of help can occur when health issues begin to overwhelm an individual, their family, and/or health care providers, such that mental health issues are missed or deemed to be a lower priority. Nonetheless, many cross-national studies have shown that older adults are in fact generally willing to seek help for mental distress, and indeed often prefer talking therapies to medication. However, they are often stymied by health professionals with inadequate knowledge and skills in terms of working with older persons.

This is unfortunate. Older adults definitely benefit greatly from receiving a variety of interventions. Psychosocial approaches, medication treatments, and combinations of the two have been shown to be effective with older adults. Although some research and meta-analyses of the psychotherapy data with older adults have shown less robust responses and/or higher relapse rates than in younger groups, in general the psychotherapy literature reflects the efficacy of talking therapies with older adults. Also, as many older adults already take numerous medications for illness, in surveys they often express a preference for psychosocial approaches to tackle mental health concerns.

A wide range of psychotherapies have amassed data on their efficacy with older persons. Although cognitive behavioural therapy approaches have been most intensively researched with older adults, data exist for the efficacy of such intervention approaches as brief psychodynamic therapy, reminiscence approaches, interpersonal therapy, and acceptance and commitment therapy. Combining psychologically informed approaches with adjunct approaches, such as exercise regimes or music therapy, has also been researched and found to have some support. The latter may be especially effective with persons experiencing cognitive declines, when more behaviourally focused, less verbal approaches may be most suitable.

Many have embraced meditation and mindfulness as the purported benefits of such activities infiltrate the mainstream. Mindfulness-based interventions to address a range of mental health coping issues have been trialled in a range of older adult populations, spanning caregivers to persons with neurological disorders such as Parkinson's disease, with mixed findings. The potential benefits of meditation and mindfulness on cognition and brain health are an exciting new area of research, if only just beginning. Researchers in this area must grapple with a host of measurement and methodological issues as this field of exploration matures.

The consequences of untreated psychiatric disorders in later life are substantial. Untreated depression and anxiety may result in increased illness or morbidity, as well as increased mortality, particularly in the case of depression. Suicide rates, particularly in older males, are of specific concern. Suicidal ideation is more prevalent in older frail persons, those experiencing chronic pain, and those with depressive symptoms or poorer social support—such populations warrant increased mental health support to avert risk of suicide.

Untreated psychiatric symptoms are associated with increased risk of some illnesses (for example, anxiety can increase the risk of coronary artery disease) and in many cases, such untreated symptoms can lead to poorer prognoses, lower compliance with recommended treatments, and suboptimal outcomes. Functional limitations may be exacerbated, thus decreasing the older adults' ability to engage in meaningful tasks and in some cases continue to live independently. Finally, untreated psychiatric symptoms and disorders lead to increased health care costs, particularly with respect to primary care settings and nursing-home facilities.

Of course, the greatest loss is to the older persons themselves, who experience increased distress, and lower quality of life and life satisfaction, when they are mentally unwell. We will return to the subject of the influence of mental health on life satisfaction and positive ageing later in this book. For now, we will turn our attention, in Chapter 4, to the social experience of ageing—social support and engagement being vital to psychological and, indeed, physical health in later life.

Chapter 4
Social and interpersonal aspects of ageing

> Grow old with me!
> The best is yet to be,
> The last of life, for which the first was made...
> (Robert Browning (1812–89))

How we interact with others, in the physical and social environment, as well as how well we cope with life events, role changes, and stresses—positive and negative (e.g. retirement; illness)—all affect how we age. By the same token, later life is intimately connected to, and affected by, circumstances and decisions occurring earlier in life, necessitating a *life course approach* for a full appreciation of ageing. As mentioned in earlier chapters, social support and engagement are critical for physical and emotional well-being. The ways in which older adults engage with younger cohorts, their contribution to the family, communities, and society more broadly, have changed over time as well as being affected by social and technological advances as diverse as the industrial revolution and Facebook. This chapter explores ageing in a social, and societal, context.

Ageing and the family

Epidemiological research suggests that most babies born since the year 2000 in France, Germany, Italy, the UK, the USA, Canada,

Japan, and other countries with long life expectancies will live to celebrate their 100th birthdays. This simple fact will have implications for family life in the coming decades, as individuals become more accustomed to multiple generations being alive at any given time, including great and great-great grandparents/ grandchildren.

In discussing family structures, the terms 'cohort' and 'generation' are frequently used. A *generation* refers to a group of people at the same step in the line of a family. In an individual family, children, parents, grandparents, and great-grandparents reflect different generations. Individuals within a generation often have specified roles and responsibilities, but these may vary between cultures, or over historical eras. For example, those in the 'parent generation' are responsible for raising their children in many cultures, but in New Zealand's Maori population, grandparents traditionally bore a large amount of child rearing responsibilities (Figure 5).

5. **Maori grandfather with grandchildren.**

This situation is not uncommon in indigenous cultures, which will be explored in more depth later in this chapter.

The term *cohort* refers to a group of people who were born during the same time period in history. Such a cohort may share formative experiences that shape attitudes, social relationships, and even biology. For example, the 'Baby Boomers' cohort (born between 1946 and 1964) experienced the years of postwar expansion, traditional values around a nuclear family structure, as well as the Vietnam era and the changing societal mores of the 1960s. The cohort born in the early part of the 20th century experienced the Great Depression, the two World Wars, and many technological advances such as commercial air travel. Such common experiences can shape a cohort's expectations of ageing, and cohorts may differ in significant ways in how they view older persons and their roles within society.

Whether speaking of generations or cohorts, there is often divergence—the so-called 'generation gap'—between age bands in terms of how ageing and the aged are viewed. Some of these differences are quite paradoxical. For example, grandchildren can profess close and caring feelings towards their grandparents, while at the same time expressing uncertainty or even antipathy towards older generations more generally. Persons of all generations profess to having an aspiration to live a long life, but may still in the course of their day consciously or unconsciously discriminate against older persons or express ageist sentiments. Sometimes the circumstances of ageing elicit mixed feelings between generations. For example, adult children helping parents with decreasing cognitive or functional abilities may endeavour to reconfigure their parent's role into a more dependent or child-like one. Research suggests that experiencing a loss of respect for their role as an adult has negative consequences for the health and well-being of the older person, and may inadvertently cause increased frustration for those in the so-called 'sandwich generation'.

Successive cohorts of individuals may experience their own lives and social connections in radically different ways depending upon societal norms and views. For example, still living today we have cohorts of individuals who have gone from experiencing the treatment of homosexuality as being a crime and an illness, with homosexuals being labelled immoral and being persecuted, to the recent wave of legal and societal recognition of same-sex marriage. These historical developments are in process now; the rights of gay individuals vary greatly across the globe, as does any one individual's acceptance in their own family, workplace, and community. Due to this cohort effect, the current generation of lesbian, gay, bisexual, and transgender (LGBT) persons in the US are more likely to live with, receive emotional support from, and rely for caregiving on friends rather than family. Internationally, much more research is warranted in this area, particularly longitudinal studies of friendship and support patterns for LGBT individuals. An important issue now emerging for LGBT persons is fear of discrimination and harassment in nursing homes; to that end, many countries are seeing more LGBT friendly or even exclusively LGBT residential retirement and aged care options becoming available.

Social class has influenced the relations between generations within a family in several ways. One's social class plays a role in survival, the higher classes being favoured through better nutrition and relatively better hygiene, better housing, and less physically demanding lifestyles, decreased chance of dying in conflicts or wars, or with (again, relatively) better access to care when ill. In the 16th century, for example, males in the English aristocracy could, after surviving to age 21, expect to live to age 71 (about 15 years longer than the average for persons in the general population who had survived until adolescence). Social class also played a role in whether multiple generations lived together, in that those in poverty often had no choice but to share a roof. From a modern perspective, there is a danger of mistakenly attributing the care in the home of older family members in earlier generations to devotion rather than economic circumstances.

It is also important to remember that younger generations in ancient as well as modern times have needed to seek assistance from parents or even grandparents due to financial or other need, meaning that assistance between generations could flow both ways. High rates of remarriage among older men in particular, throughout history, have led to blended families with complicated relationships and a wide range of ages and generations represented—more so than might be commonly thought. With increased mobility in our modern society, many more generations may at any one point be alive, yet increasingly these generations within a family may live in much more widely dispersed locations than previously. Advances in communication technologies, however, have also offered increased ways of keeping in touch with friends and family, from the telephone to Skype—in fact, older adults are the fastest growing users of Facebook.

In the 18th century, the chance of living past age 60 slowly continued to rise, resulting in older persons becoming increasingly represented in literature and art, particularly in romanticized multigenerational scenes or stories. The influence of grandparents and grandparenting is evident both in art and in historical records. At the end of the 17th century, the rising proportion of children having a living grandparent rose to the extent that the phenomena of grandparenting, and in particular of grandparents taking on some or all parenting duties, became widespread in Europe. Especially in the late 17th and into the 18th centuries, it was predominantly older female persons who were most likely to take on a primary role as a grandparent within the family, and this gendered situation continues today.

In the modern era, the incidence of grandparents assuming informal or formal responsibility for raising grandchildren is rising globally. A variety of circumstances may precipitate such caregiving arrangements—death of one or both parents of the children, substance abuse by the parents, or one or both parents being incarcerated or placed in institutional care. Particularly in countries with a high prevalence of HIV/AIDS, grandparents are often left responsible for grandchildren—UNICEF estimates that, in Eastern and Southern Africa, somewhere between 40 and 60 per cent of children orphaned due to HIV/AIDS are being cared for by grandparents. Migrants are often in a similar situation, with parents leaving their children with grandparents while they seek work in urban centres. In rural China, for example, grandparents care for 38 per cent of children under age 5 whose parents have gone to work in cities. Whether in the developed or the developing world, grandparents who assume full-time care of grandchildren face many financial and health challenges, given the demands of such care. In addition they may experience social isolation from peers, or the loss of friends, children, or partners who do not support them in their responsibilities.

Women and ageing

A digression here is warranted to discuss the particular characterization and experiences of women historically with respect to ageing, beyond their over-representation in caregiving roles. Where women are discussed in historical records, it is often in quite negative and pejorative terms. Women's beauty in youth was and is often lauded in verse and art, and the loss of beauty derided. Women have been viewed as seeking to deny the loss of their beauty through cosmetics, clothing, or other such artifice, and were often ridiculed for such efforts historically; and to a certain extent such attitudes persist today. In ancient times, women's sexuality was also of concern, particularly after the menopause, when they were seen as potentially less restrained in their sexual appetites and generally vulnerable to the effects of what were viewed as the toxic humours associated with menstruation (of which they were unable to rid themselves after menopause). Again, in the modern era aspects of older women's sexuality remain either taboo or discounted. Women, especially poorer women in reduced circumstances and without family, were also more likely in the Middle Ages to be accused of witchcraft.

These generally negative views of women and their role in society were balanced historically by the view that women might gain greater independence after age 60. This was especially true in the Middle Ages, when widows could manage their own affairs, and were able to take on more public responsibilities, for example as midwives or adjudicators in delicate matters such as sexual behaviours or matrimonial concerns. Older women were also seen as physically less 'female' in nature and hence more capable of reason, and as such due greater respect than younger women.

Today women throughout the world face similar challenges to those faced historically, even if they are also embracing new opportunities. The 2007 WHO report 'Women, Ageing and Health', which again takes a life course perspective, highlights both societal and cultural effects on women's health and well-being earlier in life. It shows how restrictions on education, inadequate access to decent work due to gender discrimination in the labour force, and domestic violence, which may begin early in life and which later in life is a common form of elder abuse, all have an influence on their health and well-being later in life. Policy imperatives to improve older women's health and income security include ensuring equal rights to the inheritance of property and resources upon the death of a partner, and ensuring equal access to healthcare.

Ageing in communities and societies

Amid rising standards of living for older people, there is still wide variation between countries in the developed and the developing world with respect to the living standards of older persons. Worldwide, however, older women, particularly widows, show a higher incidence of poverty. Older persons in minority groups and those living in regional or remote areas also tend to suffer disproportionately from poverty and poorer living conditions.

The United Nations Development Programme publishes an annual report on human development, which includes ageing issues and concerns. In their report a theme from the beginning of this chapter, that early circumstances in life form the backdrop to later years, is highlighted, in that vulnerabilities in older populations often represent lifelong vulnerabilities and adverse circumstances. For example, the report notes that 46 per cent of people over 60 globally live with a disability, often continuing from earlier ages. The report also stresses the underutilization of human capital represented by older persons. This mismatch between increasing longevity and reduced opportunities for social participation has been exacerbated in recent years by widening gaps between the quality and, in many places, the quantity of life in later years between developed and developing countries. In Organization for Economic Co-operation and Development (OECD) countries the poverty rate tends to be higher for older people than for the population as a whole, and higher for older women than for older men. Social policy, at the level of local communities through to nations, will need to better address strategies to improve well-being for older persons, including greater social participation and stronger welfare provision for those with the greatest needs.

UN Development Programme report, 2014

Both the UN and WHO have published important statements and policy initiatives with respect to ageing, which act as guidelines for national policies, cross-national research, and political efforts to better support ageing. The UN 'Principles for Older Persons' (which cover independence, participation, care, self-fulfilment, and dignity) and the WHO report 'Global Health and Aging' are two of the more important of these documents. Such policies are aimed at increasing older adults' meaningful participation in all aspects of all societies globally. Many organizations, as well as governments, have put in place statements addressing the rights of older persons, or goals to improve income security and increase health and well-being among older people. For example, the 2002 Madrid International Plan of Action on Aging (MIPAA) states that older persons must be included in development and social service planning of communities and nations. In 2012, the United Nations Population Fund, in collaboration with HelpAge International, published an update of progress on the MIPAA goals and included more directly the voices of older adults globally relating their life circumstances. Health and income security were cited as areas still requiring urgent policy attention, particularly considering the increasing economic and social burden of dementia globally. However, the benefits contributed by older persons to society, in terms of caregiving, volunteering, participating in civic and other organizations, entrepreneurial endeavours, and so forth, were found to be substantial and growing, particularly in societies where the contribution of older persons was recognized, supported, and valued.

What do older people themselves think about ageing? HelpAge International, a global organization examining the ageing experience locally, particularly in the developing world, has conducted a survey of 1,265 people in thirty-two countries across Africa, Asia, Europe, and the Caribbean. In their survey, 48 per cent of respondents felt the world is getting better for older persons, while 29 per cent thought the situation was getting worse. Of note is the fact that 72 per cent of older persons living in rural areas felt valued compared to only 56 per cent in urban areas. With respect to health and resources, 63 per cent of respondents found it hard to access healthcare when required, and 72 per cent of respondents reported their income did not cover basic services such as water, electricity, food, or adequate housing.

Culture and ageing

Most of the increase in older people in the coming decades will be in developing nations. Unfortunately, across these developing countries health outcomes are poorer than for more developed countries, and are generally poorer for women across countries. The WHO Study on Global Aging and Adult Health (SAGE) involves an attempt to track health outcomes for persons over 50 in nationally representative cohorts of respondents in six countries (China, Ghana, India, Mexico, Russia, and South Africa). The overall health status scores in these countries place Chinese males and females with the highest scores; and Indian males and females with the lowest scores. The health status of both males and females declines sharply in all six countries from early to late life. Over time these data will help with policy and planning initiatives. In particular, the SAGE study focuses on health risks faced by older people, and assesses how these risks affect current and future disability, so that appropriate prevention and intervention services may be targeted.

Culturally, responses to ageing differ widely. A commonly cited difference in cultural perspectives is between the more individualistic cultures in Europe and North America and the more collectivist cultures in Asia, South America, and Indigenous societies. For example, the Confucian traditions of filial piety and familism remain strong in many Asian countries as well as in their corresponding migrant communities worldwide; these traditions influence healthcare choices in later life, including the choice of residential aged care as a care option for elderly parents. However, increasing Western influences in these countries, and increasing incidences of small, nuclear families with women in full-time employment, have affected some traditional aspects of collectivist culture.

Indigenous peoples make up about 6 per cent of the world's population and increasingly policy and practice approaches for older adults in such societies are being developed in cooperation with Indigenous communities. Unfortunately, in all countries Indigenous peoples have poorer health outcomes, lower life expectancies, and greater barriers to accessing healthcare for all age groups, particularly older adults. Worldwide, older Indigenous women have the highest levels of illiteracy, even in countries with relatively high literacy rates. Increased exposure to risk factors early in life contribute to poorer health later in life for many Indigenous people. For example, Aboriginal people in Australia experience the onset of dementia ten to fifteen years earlier than non-Aboriginal Australians. This is due to a range of factors including lower levels of education, poorer access to healthcare, increased exposure to chronic illnesses such as diabetes, and earlier life events such as head trauma and stroke. Increased research on the prevalence of dementia and other disorders of later life is urgently needed in Indigenous populations who, despite generally poorer health outcomes, are continuing to experience gains in longevity and hence have increasing service needs for their older cohorts.

In many cultures, including Indigenous cultures, older adults occupy a place where they are respected for their knowledge and experience, and are expected to pass their knowledge down to younger generations. Jared Diamond, in his book *The World Until Yesterday* (2012) makes the point that, in many traditional cultures without written text, older individuals were valued for knowledge on how to cope with unexpected circumstances (for example, where to find food or shelter in case of natural disasters, which might only occur once in a generation). However, the advent of written histories to some extent supplanted the role of the older person as a repository of knowledge in these societies. Research today continues to show that older adults often have a superior coping response in the face of disasters, natural or otherwise, than younger groups—and so the support and stability they may lend a group is still very much of value.

The diversity of cultural backgrounds and increasing numbers of older people have implications for providing culturally appropriate care services and information for this group, and require a work force with knowledge of and sensitivities to the intersection of ageing, culture, and physical and mental health issues, particularly in nursing-home settings. Worldwide, the median age of international migrants is 38.4 years, compared with a median global average age of 29.2 years. This pattern holds across all continents, though the ages vary, with Europe having the older general population and Africa the youngest. Migrants as a group tend generally to suffer increased mental health problems coupled with increased barriers to accessing mental health services (e.g. financial and language issues). Patients who suffer from dementia often lose a second language and revert to their first language, causing difficulties in providing adequate care for them in nursing-home settings.

One common factor across cultures is the experience of feeling younger than one's chronological age, which has been demonstrated in several studies internationally. Also, the older one is, the greater the gap between one's actual age and how old one feels. Typically, after age 65 people generally feel about ten years younger than their chronological age. Despite varying context and circumstances, largely individual factors—particularly physical and mental well-being, both objective and subjective—contribute to one's subjectively imagined age. Finally, a longitudinal study found that the higher the person's subjective age the higher their chance of experiencing poor health and higher mortality, even after adjusting for multiple potential contributing factors. In other words, the closer our perceived and actual ages are, the worse off we are likely to be.

Wealth and retirement in later life

Old age as a life stage has been linked to benefits tied to achieving a certain age. The German chancellor, Otto von Bismarck, initiated the first national pension scheme in the late 1880s. Initially the age of retirement in Germany was set at 70, but a few decades later this fell to the more familiar age of 65. The initial age was set not as is sometimes mooted because lifespan was lower than age 70, but because, as has been alluded to previously, adult workers at that time who had survived past adolescence could reasonably expect to live to age 70 (if not much beyond that age). Such retirement pension programmes have since proliferated in many other countries, and can differ in small and large ways. Some pensions are state-funded while others are employment-based, and they may entail varying levels of contributions from individuals. Usually (but not always) the retirement age—when a pension may be accessed—differs for men and women, due in part to differences in expected mortality.

Increasing industrialization, urbanization, and population growth in the 19th century affected persons of all ages, including older adults. The diminished security of work in an increasingly industrialized society meant that many older persons, particularly from lower socioeconomic backgrounds, often faced unemployment and reduced circumstances. Industrialization and the work created from this movement were more intolerant of age-related infirmities than the more agricultural or craft industries had been. Yet for those with greater financial resources, their later years might be free of the need to work, affording them leisure time in which to pursue interests—whether due to a pension or accumulated wealth. Then as now, the ability to enjoy one's retirement was tied to both health and resources, although autonomy, irrespective of resources, has always figured prominently in older persons' goals in later life. As Cicero (Roman, 107–44 BCE) proclaims:

> Old age will only be respected if it fights for itself, maintains its rights, avoids dependence on anyone and asserts control over its own to its last breath.

Older persons can expect a varying number of years in retirement, affected by many factors. Across OECD countries, expected years in retirement for men varies—for example, in 2007, men in France could expect twenty-four years in retirement; whereas in Mexico, men could only expect just over nine years of retirement (in 2007 the OECD average was 18.1 years, with the USA trending just below this figure on average). There are also many cross-national differences between effective age of retirement and a country's official age of retirement, as demonstrated in Figure 6.

In the modern era, poverty and poor quality of life remain a reality for many older adults globally, in part because despite the increased number of retirement schemes in some countries, approximately 80 per cent of the world's older population does not receive a pension, and instead relies upon work or family for

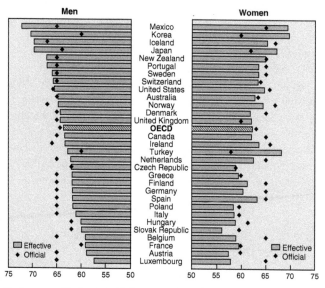

6. Average effective age of labour-market exit and normal pensionable age.

income support. Again, earlier vulnerabilities follow into older age, and with each passing decade, persons experience a reduced likelihood of escape from poverty. Illness and disability, and loss of a partner, also more likely in later life, again reduce income and financial circumstances. Reliance on the state or family reduces autonomy, increases stress, and may lead to an increased perception of the older person as a burden, even in his or her own eyes. However, both contributory and non-contributory pension schemes improve financial security and resilience in later life.

Post-retirement employment is now the subject of increasing research. In many studies, research suggests that abrupt retirement, whether due to illness or disability, as opposed to a planned exit from the workforce while in good health, often results in decreased satisfaction and well-being. So-called 'bridge employment', part-time work following full-time employment, in the same or a different job, tends to result in better outcomes in terms of reported satisfaction and well-being. In addition, keeping actively engaged by volunteering or mentoring others, whether in one's field of prior employment or in other settings (e.g. an NGO; in a community service organization) can assist with adjustment to retirement and satisfaction, as well as quality of life, post-full-time employment. Particularly in developed countries, the Baby Boomer generation is signalling an increasing desire to continue working into their later years. The increased sense of autonomy and time flexibility mentioned earlier has been cited in recent research as being behind the finding that both part-time work as well as everyday leisure activities are enjoyed more post-retirement.

Care of older persons: historical and cultural perspectives

Intergenerational reciprocity has typically been the norm across history with respect to the care parents afford children early in life and the care children are expected to extend to parents in their later years. Such stipulations exist in records from ancient times, often with the proviso that if parents had not cared well for their children (specified in such ways as 'having taught them a trade'), then they could not expect their children to look after them in old age. Within such arrangements, in the ancient as well as the modern world, there are balances that need to be struck between being completely independent in old age but without a safety net of care should it be required, and being under the control of one's children to an excessive extent.

Support (or lack thereof) of older adults by children as well as by the state has fluctuated through history and also has varied by culture. We have already touched on legislation in China requiring the provision of care by children for their parents, to ensure the latter's bodily and interpersonal well-being. In Singapore, children who cannot financially support their ageing parents must make a public declaration of this fact before the state will step in with assistance—and many older adults would rather live in reduced circumstances than suffer loss of face though such a public announcement. India and Israel both have regulations regarding adult children's obligation to provide care and shelter for elderly parents who lack the resources to be self-sufficient. Brazil and South Africa have policies that explicitly state that older people should reside with family (or independently) for as long as possible before seeking institutional care.

Residing with family is not without some risk in the case of older adults. The WHO reports that approximately one in ten older people globally experiences abuse every month, and elder abuse is for some the final stage of a long experience of abuse at the hands of a spouse. In one Australian study, the single greatest risk of financial abuse for an older person is having had children. However, despite abuse sometimes occurring within family settings, the WHO reports that in many countries rates of elder abuse are higher for those living in institutions than for those in the community. Global data on elder abuse are still inadequate to give a full picture of the extent of the problem, particularly in institutional settings in developing countries; more research on this issue globally is required. However, from what we know, depression, anxiety, and post-traumatic stress are the most common consequences of elder abuse, and emotional abuse often leads to greater psychological distress than physical abuse.

Care and care provision are also tied to living circumstances. Older persons often prefer to 'age in place'—to remain in familiar surroundings, as they grow older. However, this may not be tenable for a variety of reasons. For example, the older adult may have physical or mental illnesses that make care in the home impractical or unsafe. Changed or reduced circumstances may make maintaining the home unviable. Nonetheless, family often do step in to offer care so that the older person can remain in their home for longer; or the older person may move into the home of one of their children, or another family member, willing to provide care and a place to live. Institutionalization is often thought of by the older person and their family and loved ones as a last resort. Here too, serious physical or mental conditions may make care by professional staff in such a supported medical environment necessary.

The beliefs and attitudes of older adults towards institutionalized nursing-home care are complex. Many older adults do not want to be a burden on their family and so may view entering a nursing home as the lesser of two evils. Indeed, a qualitative study in New Zealand showed that many of the older persons in their survey felt that medical practices to extend life may not be desirable for a variety of reasons, including increasing the burden on family and loved ones. Although many studies of middle-aged and young-old persons demonstrate a marked preference for ageing 'in place', a Swedish study of persons over 80 revealed a more complex picture of preferences in living arrangements. In this qualitative study the urge to remain in one's familiar home was spurred by attachment to home and neighbourhood as well as to familiar habits and routines. In contrast, decreasing ability to perform basic activities of living combined with increasingly poor health, including having dementia, can precipitate the decision to move into institutionalized care, while inability to maintain a large home or the wish to increase one's social circle might induce a move to a different or smaller place of residence. In this study, one reason put forward reflected desires beyond the independence of living in one's home, incorporating the therapeutic value of caring for hearth and home:

> Sometimes I think it is a little lonely in the house, but at the same time, the garden and house, well, they provide me with a little therapy, because I feel I can cope with a lot and do a lot myself...
>
> (Löfqvist et al. 2013: 922)

Circumstances pushing (e.g. ill health) or pulling (e.g. seeking more social contact) older adults to consider relocation, coupled with increasing numbers of older adults who choose or are forced to consider relocation, have spurred an ever-expanding range of living arrangements on offer. The familiar choice of moving to a retirement community or to a nursing home has been augmented by these expanding choices. For example, the Abbeyfield model of senior accommodation, started in the UK but now expanded to many other countries including Australia, is more like a house- or flat-sharing option familiar to residents of Commonwealth countries. A number of residents (usually around ten) share a large house with public living and dining areas, and a live-in housekeeper provides some meals, and cleans and maintains the public areas of the home. Other innovative housing options for seniors in a variety of countries include intergenerational housing arrangements (for example, with some rooms for students and others for seniors) or communities designed to hark back to earlier eras (for example, communities with a 1950s theme). In the Netherlands an entire village, including shops and recreational facilities, has been created to provide a safe environment for those with dementia.

Various nations have systematic strategies in place to assist older adults to age 'in place'. Japan's Long-term Care Insurance fund compensates homeowners for home adaptations to help with independent living. France pays an allowance to older persons wishing to acquire technical devices and aids to ensure continued autonomy. Singapore extends housing subsidies to families who take an apartment in the same building as an ageing parent. An innovative home share scheme in Melbourne, Australia, matches young people with older adults to share living space; the younger person does light housekeeping chores in exchange for reduced or free rent.

The importance of social interaction in later life

We have reviewed much evidence on the benefits of social engagement in later life. Social ties with friends and family have important benefits for physical and psychological health. Likewise, social identity theory informs us of the importance of group membership in our sense of who we are, with group membership possibly also having protective and restorative health benefits.

We know from Laura Carstensen's work on 'socioemotional selectivity theory and the positivity effect' that later in life, despite a shrinking social network, older individuals manage to derive as great if not greater social benefits from their social connections. Moreover, because older adults realize that they have lived more of their life than they have yet to live, they are more likely to seek meaningful engagement in their activities and social relationships, to make the best use of their time remaining.

Sexuality and its expression is an important part of ageing. It has been mentioned that in a variety of ages and contexts, intimacy in later life was denigrated or neglected. Now, although ageist stereotypes persist, presenting later life as asexual or sexual desire in later life as unacceptable, research has demonstrated the value of intimacy for older persons. The positive effect of having a partner in later life on one's health and emotional well-being has been demonstrated across countries. While longer term partnerships are more frequently studied, recently the development of new romantic relationships in later life has been the subject of research. For example, older adults who develop new relationships are more likely to be seeking companionship and sexual activity, and less likely to be interested in progressing to cohabitation or marriage than younger cohorts. Later life may reduce gender differences in the experience of love and intimacy, and both men and women report that their romantic partnerships improve with age. Maintaining independence, economic factors, the influence of family and friends, and healthcare concerns are some of the factors that shape romantic relationships in later life. This has led to the phenomenon of living-apart-together (LAT), a type of relationship choice also more popular with older than with younger adults. This is not of course to say that romance in later life is strictly practical—infatuation, betrayal, and enduring love are to be found here as they are in earlier life stages. Both qualitative and quantitative research with older adults emphasizes their continued interest in engaging with romantic partners who share interests and values, and with whom they can share personally and sexually fulfilling relationships.

Finally, we know the profound, potentially negative consequences that social isolation (lack of social contact) and loneliness (perceived lack of social connectedness leading to negative feelings) have on older adults in terms of increased risks for poor mental health, cognitive impairment and dementia, and poorer physical health. There is evidence from many quarters that interventions to reduce social isolation (by increasing and improving social connections) and addressing feelings stemming from loneliness, particularly through psychosocial interventions, result in positive gains in physical and mental health and well-being.

There are many recommendations for pursuing healthy ageing; among these the importance of maintaining social connections and engagement is underscored. But particularly for vulnerable older adults, those who are frail or have limited mobility, who are socially disadvantaged or suffer from mental health issues, or who are in nursing homes or other institutions, social connectedness is difficult to actualize. In my experience as a clinician, often these individuals experience pure social interactions at a greatly reduced rate—these being often primarily with healthcare professionals around healthcare needs. Simple conversation is in desperately short supply! And even for relatively healthy, community-dwelling older persons, the frequency of meaningful social interactions may be far less than desired. Perhaps, like the minimum daily requirement of essential nutrients for our physical bodies, there is a minimum dose of social interactions required to maintain well-being. (We certainly know this is true for infants and children at the start of life.) Ensuring and facilitating receipt of such regular meaningful social interactions may be one of the most powerful tools we possess to improve the lives of older persons, as individuals and as a society. Given increasing longevity worldwide, there is an imperative to examine how we can advise older adults to age well, and as a society promote positive and successful ageing—the subject of Chapter 5.

Chapter 5
Positive and successful ageing

> And yet the wiser mind
> Mourns less for what age takes away
> Than what it leaves behind.
>   (William Wordsworth (1770–1850))

Positive and successful ageing, in terms of physical, mental, and social well-being in later life, are the focus of this chapter. Current findings and directions in research, interventions, and social policy with respect to positive and successful ageing are addressed. Although both positive and less positive aspects of the ageing process have been acknowledged since ancient times, ageing research has only focused more strongly on health and well-being, rather than disease and disability, in the last few decades. Now attention has turned to those who have survived to an advanced age, and how those who continue to be active and engaged in this latter portion of their lives have achieved this. Studies of the benefits of thinking and acting in positive ways, often for the benefit of others, have yielded important and encouraging results. Successful ageing is now the subject of policy frameworks, lifespan theories of development, and actions large and small affecting older adults globally.

Key determinants to successful ageing

The word 'health' has its origins in the old English word 'hoelth', meaning a state of being sound; the term was generally used to infer soundness of the body. The WHO's definition of active ageing is 'the process of optimizing opportunities for health, participation and security in order to enhance quality of life as people age' (WHO 2002: 12). This definition echoes an older definition of health, as put forward by Australian Aboriginal peoples, who feel that, 'Health does not just mean the physical well-being of the individual but refers to the social, emotional, spiritual and cultural well-being of the whole community. This is a whole of life view and includes the cyclical concept of life-death-life' (NH&MRC 1995: 4). While such definitions might be at risk of reducing all states of experience to an origin in physical health, they also reflect the now widely accepted empirical findings of intricate interconnections between physical, cognitive, emotional, and social well-being.

As mentioned in previous chapters, the WHO has published several key policy documents on health and well-being in later life. The WHO Active Aging Policy Framework (2002) has been influential in shaping the conversation around healthy and successful ageing. The word 'active' was specifically chosen to reflect older adults' continuing participation in the social, economic, cultural, spiritual, and civic affairs of their communities. Such participation and engagement are key determinants thought to contribute to ageing well. These individual determinants of active ageing are viewed as influenced by cross-cutting determinants of ageing well, such as culture and gender. Both culture and gender shape how individuals and societies view older individuals and the ageing process. From a lifespan perspective, effects of these determinants earlier in life can have an impact on health and well-being in later life. Nevertheless, in the latter portion of life, individuals and societies can work to ensure that health and social services, the physical environment, and personal, behavioural, economic, and social determinants (which figure as key determinants of active ageing) are supported. This in turn will assist the older individual to maximize participation and enjoyment of life.

The importance of health promotion, disease prevention, and equitable access to primary healthcare, mental healthcare, as well as long-term care has already been discussed in earlier chapters. Poor oral health has not yet been mentioned, and remains a contributor to several other systemic health issues (such as cardiovascular health), and can cause pain, poor health, and reduced quality of life in later years. As such, oral care, as well as other key health issues with broad impact, particularly in the developing world, such as cataracts and other illnesses of the eyes leading to near or total blindness, are a focus of WHO global health programmes. Genetics and epigenetics, as well as psychological, economic, and social factors, are other important aspects of health, which are highlighted in the WHO Active Aging Framework.

Lifestyle factors, including modifying behaviour when necessary, are key to active ageing and the focus of a large empirical literature. Physical activity in support of physical and mental health is increasingly emerging as a key element of health maintenance as well as supporting independent living in later life. Maintaining physical activity as well as minimizing periods of inactivity is consistently supported as improving health across the lifespan, including late life. Healthy eating encompasses healthy nutrition with the aim of avoiding either malnutrition or overeating, and issues around food security as well as obesity remain particular concerns for older adults living in poverty. Diets high in saturated fats, salt, and sugar, and low in fibre, fruits, and vegetables, are major risk factors for a number of chronic conditions in later life such as diabetes, cardiovascular disease, arthritis, and some cancers, with the potential (such as via poor cardiovascular health) to in turn increase the risk for conditions such as dementia.

Excessive consumption of alcohol and use of tobacco products have been shown to have detrimental effects on health and well-being at all points in the lifespan, including later life. Medication side effects and polypharmacy may have iatrogenic effects on health. Older adults often have decreased tolerances for medications, which are cleared from the body at slower rates than in younger individuals. Multiple medications and poorer clearance rates can result in higher rates of negative medication interaction effects. Adverse but common drug side effects include declines in thinking ability and increased falls (especially associated with sleeping pills and benzodiazepines—a familiar form of which is valium). There is emerging data on the risk of stroke as well as Parkinsonian side effects from antipsychotic medications prescribed to address psychological and behavioural symptoms of dementia.

The physical environment has a large role to play in health in later life. Age-friendly environments can assist older adults to maintain independence, remain mobile and able to pursue activities and goals, and pursue engagement with the wider society. The WHO age-friendly cities programme looks at how urban areas large and small can enhance the living experience of their older citizens. This network includes cities large and small in the Americas, Africa, Eastern Mediterranean, Europe, Southeast Asia, and the Western Pacific. A bottom-up participatory approach to enhancing age-friendliness involves older adults analysing concerns and potential solutions and passing these on to inform government policies. Successful urban planning for older adults often proves useful to people of all ages. However, age-friendly environments go beyond transportation, assistive services, housing, and civic spaces that are welcoming and supportive of older persons. Such environments also combat ageism, encourage civic participation, embody respect and social inclusion, and embrace healthy and active ageing principles in their planning and execution.

What do older adults themselves think are the key ingredients to ageing successfully? A number of cross-cultural reviews of surveys of older individuals have found that older adults think about successful ageing in much the same way as the researchers and policymakers who have contributed to the WHO active ageing policy. Older adults generally take a more holistic view of ageing well, incorporating aspects of physical and emotional health, as well as social and functional domains. Although cultural and gender differences emerge from such cross-cultural investigations, overall the similarities in views shared by older people outweigh their differences.

Health literacy in general is a large topic of research for persons of all ages, and older adults have also been the subject of studies and interventions in this area. Health literacy is affected in part by the individual's skills and abilities to make sense of health information, and act upon it. However, the other key component is the health literacy environment, from healthcare professionals through to policies in place regarding health, and the healthcare information available to groups and individuals. Lower rates of health literacy have been associated with decreased physical and mental well-being, and increased morbidity and mortality, in older persons. Sociodemographic factors associated with higher rates of health literacy include higher levels of educational attainment and intact cognition, particularly memory. There is some evidence from longitudinal studies that health literacy declines with age, but as successive cohorts are able to access information from multiple sources including social media and the internet this picture may change. Interventions for improving health literacy in various age groups, but particularly in older adults, lags behind the literature documenting the negative impact of poor health literacy.

How do older adults' views of the external world change over time? The *positivity effect* describes the tendency for older adults to attend to and remember positive affect and stimuli, more so than younger adults. Interestingly, and in a refutation of the hypothesis that this might be due to degraded neural networks with increasing age, the positivity effect appears strongest in older adults who appear the most intact cognitively. International data on how such theories apply in cross-cultural contexts is a growing area of research. For example, the positivity effect does not hold uniformly across cultures. This effect has been replicated extensively in Western populations, but only partially in Eastern cultures. In Asian cultural contexts the values of harmony and equilibrium are placed at a higher premium than happiness, which may influence how persons from these cultures attend to and encode stimuli. This also draws attention to the difficulty in measuring emotions and their desirability across cultures. It will be fascinating in the coming decades to track changes within these cultures in terms of successful ageing.

Successful and positive ageing

Rowe and Kahn (1998), in their book *Successful Aging*, define positive ageing as the ability to sustain three important characteristics and behaviours, namely a low risk of disease and disease-related disability, a high level of physical and mental functioning, and active engagement with life. Other authors have added such diverse criteria as social competence and productivity, personal control, and life satisfaction to this equation of healthy or productive ageing. However, due to researchers having varying definitions of successful ageing, varying ages of participants (particularly higher proportions of young-old versus oldest old), as well as varying objective and subjective input and outcome measures, the proportion of older persons classified as 'successfully ageing' varies enormously, from 3 per cent to 95 per cent, as reported in a review on the topic. This is a relatively recent field of study, one that will no doubt continue to grow in coming years.

Yet despite its status as a relatively new field, many intriguing findings on successful ageing have been reported. A recent focus of interest in the field involves research on the impact of meaningful engagement on activities and interpersonal relationships. Volunteering is an important role for some older adults, one which research supports as contributing to positive health and well-being. Volunteering may particularly benefit older persons who are more isolated or who experience declining informal social contact. Volunteering can improve social contact as well as provide engagement in a meaningful activity, and has been shown to have positive effects on self-rated health, mood, increased life satisfaction, lower levels of functional dependence, and even decreased mortality. A particular form of volunteering, in mentoring at-risk or early career populations, has also been studied with respect to older adults and found to generally contribute positively to ageing, particularly with respect to engagement in a meaningful and valued activity. Volunteering by senior citizens also of course benefits those served by the myriad organizations in which such volunteering occurs. Organizations that target the skills of older volunteers are also increasing in number. Advocacy, mentoring, teaching, and leadership are just some of the roles in which older adults can exercise their talents and knowledge.

The positive psychology movement of recent years has also contributed to research on ageing. Martin Seligman, a psychologist, has championed the study of 'human flourishing' and an applied approach to optimal functioning, and this goal has been applied to later life. Seligman's (2003) 'Authentic Happiness Theory' posits three key facets to positive mental health and well-being: the pleasurable life (positive emotions), the engaged life (flow and mindfulness), and the meaningful life (meaning and purpose). In 2011, Seligman revised his theory to include two additional components: positive relationships and accomplishments.

Positive psychology interventions such as keeping a gratitude journal and engaging in acts of altruism (reflecting the meaningful life) have been shown to improve mental health and quality of life in older adults, even in those who are ill or functionally disabled. For example, older adults who volunteered to give massages to infants in care showed lowered levels of stress hormones and biological indications of enhanced immune system functioning. Volunteering and mentoring, already discussed, would also fit this aspect of positive engagement in meaningful activities, as well as contribute to positive relationships and accomplishments.

Although the pleasurable life has sometimes been equated to more fleeting or ephemeral life experiences (such as enjoying a good meal), leisure activities may be thought of as encompassing pure pleasurable experiences as well as adding meaning and engagement to life. Study of leisure or discretionary activities has taken several paths with respect to older persons. Benefits of participation in such leisure activities include improvements in physical and mental health, life satisfaction, and social relationships, as well as being a protective factor against dementia in several studies. An influential study by Verghese and colleagues in the *New England Journal of Medicine* in 2003 found that a number of leisure activities, such as reading, playing board games, playing musical instruments, and dancing were associated with a lower risk of dementia. And a Scandinavian study of leisure activities, where such activities were sorted into categories of cognitive and/or physical and/or social, found that greater health benefits accrued to individuals who engaged in leisure activities encompassing two or more of these domains.

What about older people's own sense of their well-being and happiness? Across a number of research and national surveys and both longitudinal and cross-cultural studies, older adults over age 65 report in general less psychological distress, and greater happiness and positive emotions, and, in a US study, less stress, worry, and anger than middle aged and younger respondents. A sense of purpose in life and engagement in meaningful interpersonal relationships are some of the factors likely to increase happiness and life satisfaction in the later years.

Psychological development in the second half of life

Many developmental theories give only minimal coverage to development over the entire lifespan. For example, Erik Erikson's psychosocial stages are among the best known developmental theories. Although proposed as a lifespan model of development, only three of Erikson's eight stages occur after adolescence and life post-65 is covered by a single stage: maturity. In contrast, Gene Cohen's life stages theory emphasizes growth and development throughout the middle and later years. His theory encompasses developmental milestones just as important as those of Piaget concerning early childhood development. However, Cohen's stages tackle issues such as striving to give meaning to life; wishing to repair relationships and achieve greater harmony in interpersonal networks; giving back to society through mentoring or legacy projects such as philanthropic gifts or foundations; and passing on knowledge through writing personal or family histories. The key is the pursuit of meaning, often through creative means.

What do these stages (or 'phases', in Cohen's terminology) look like? First, unlike many theories of development, Cohen's phases have a great deal of overlap and do not necessarily represent an invariant or fixed progression. So people can skip phases or experience these phases in an order other than that presented—Cohen was aware of and wished to cater for the great heterogeneity in the experience of older persons. His first phase is *midlife evaluation* and comes at a time (from early 40s to late 50s) when people first confront their mortality (similar to Carstensen's SST and the recognition of having a finite amount of time left to live). People in this phase have their actions shaped by a desire to re-evaluate or explore their life more fully, although sometimes this phase may be driven by crisis. The second phase, *liberation*, experienced during the late 50s to early 70s, is characterized by an 'if not now, when?' push to speak one's mind and act according to one's needs, and often involves experimentation and innovation. The third phase, *summing up*, usually occurs from the late 60s through to the 80s, and involves a desire to share wisdom and experiences, and to find meaning in a re-examination and summing up of their life led to that point. The fourth and final phase, *encore*, usually experienced from the late 70s to the end of life, is a time of reflection and celebration, with a desire to live well to the end while continuing to explore variations on lifelong pursuits and interests. Cohen thought that these stages in later life mapped onto activities and pursuits, such as mentoring, constructing genealogies, and initiating legacy activities. The drive towards interest in such activities, in Cohen's view, both reflected later life stages of development as well as neuronal changes in the brain (such as the enhanced connectivity of the corpus callosum), which underpinned and supported movement through these life stages.

In addition to putting forward these life stages, Cohen proposed constructing a 'social portfolio' in one's later years, to ensure reaping the maximum social benefits in the face of uncertain conditions. The idea is taken from the notion of a balanced financial portfolio being required to ensure income security in later life, with protection built in for unexpected events. In Cohen's social portfolio, activities engaged in with others should be balanced by activities one can engage in by oneself. Also, in a nod to the strong literature on the benefits of physical activity in ageing well, vigorous activities should be balanced by those that are not as physically demanding. In this way, in the face of events associated with increasing age, such as the loss of family and friends to illness and death, and the potential for sudden or gradual loss of physical functioning, a range of activities that have meaning for the individual will still be available.

Creativity plays a large role in how older adults express themselves in Cohen's developmental phases. But often creativity has been portrayed in the past as declining in later life—such portrayals could be argued to still influence thinking about creativity and ageing today. For example, one author, Harvey Lehman, presented his 'Peak and Decline Model' with an entire book (*Age and Achievement*, 1953) devoted to graphs showing that, in a wide range of fields of human endeavour, people did not create significant works past their 30s, in most fields, including the arts and sports. This seems a distressing and less than positive finding. But again, we need to take into account lifespan (as well perhaps as the social era in which Lehman wrote). If the long-lived person has a longer time to contribute then they will naturally contribute at many stages in their life, but short-lived people can only contribute at early stages. Moreover, what is gauged as 'important' is often early works, whereas critics may be more reticent about judging later works. More recent research has revealed peaks in creativity and productivity at multiple points in the lifespan, including later life, and particularly in the more creative and artistic fields. In keeping with Cohen's model of later life creativity, over the last decade researchers have explored the evolution of creativity over the lifespan, how positive and negative changes in cognition and personality might influence creativity in older persons, and how changes in the environment might influence creativity and generativity in later years.

Another way of looking at creativity is that different types of creativity manifest at different stages in life. For example, children are often creative, perhaps in part because they have not yet internalized many societal norms. Later when a career is mastered, rules may become more readily apparent, and the older person may have the courage, prestige, or sheer determination to break or modify them. Openness to new experiences, having protected time to engage in creative ideas, and living in a supportive environment allowing creative expression are important for achieving creative potential. However, stereotypes about declines in creativity or ability with age can inhibit productivity and creativity in the later years. For example, research by Levy and Langer demonstrated that acceptance of the stereotypes of old age as representing a time of loss can itself worsen memory performance and self-efficacy in older people.

Resilience and wisdom

The simultaneous co-existence of a multitude of accumulating decrements in health and functionality with the robust finding that self-reported happiness and well-being improves in the latter portion of life has sometimes been labelled the 'paradox of ageing'. It appears as though, despite such declines, older adults are for the most part more content in later life than in previous stages of life—a finding that has held true for most cross-sectional as well as longitudinal research. For example, in the large US Successful Aging Evaluation (SAGE) study, after adjusting for age, a higher self-rating of successful ageing was associated with higher education levels, better cognitive functioning, better perceived physical and mental health, a reduced amount of depression, and greater optimism and resilience (Figure 7).

Resilience, meaning broadly an individual's adaptation to stress and adversity, is a construct researched throughout the lifespan, including later life. Resilience is usually studied at the individual level, and instances of older adults' resilience in the face of natural disasters, and the relationship between higher levels of resilience and well-being in later life, have already been mentioned. But resilience can also operate at a group level, and can be measured

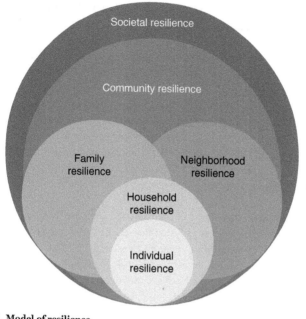

7. **Model of resilience.**

at the level of households, families, neighbourhoods, communities, and societies. In Figure 7, Wild and colleagues (2013) highlight not only these conceptualizations of resilience but also the differing scales of resilience that impact on older adults' ability to cope with adverse circumstances.

Such social resilience is an important construct, recognizing the interrelations between individual and collective resources, which may be more important in later years, particularly for more dependent or frail elders. Models of resilience need to distinguish between various areas of life, where older persons may have greater or lesser degrees of personal mastery, resources, coping skills, or external support. In turn, individual aspects of resilience may intersect and be enhanced or weakened by the resilience of the family, community, or society.

Protective factors for enhanced coping and resilience in the face of stress include individual factors such as optimism, personal control, coping skills and positive self-rated health, as well as familial and community resources such as quantity and quality of positive social support. Perceiving oneself as having control (either objective or subjective) and a sense of self-efficacy are important for resilience. Unfortunately internal factors such as poor physical or mental health and external factors such as ageism and lack of social support can erode the resilience of older persons.

Wisdom is another aspect of ageing increasingly studied, but with a long tradition of more philosophical enquiry. Wisdom is evident in writings from ancient to modern times. Epicurus (341–270 BCE) declared, 'Search for wisdom, you shall drink from an inexhaustible well for the health of the soul.' Einstein (1879–1955) opined, 'Wisdom is not a product of schooling, but of the lifelong attempt to acquire it.'

Paul Baltes and other geropsychologists at the Max Planck Institute of Berlin have embarked on a decades-long exploration of wisdom, particularly in later life. They have defined wisdom as representing an expert knowledge system reliant upon various types of knowledge and experience relating to fundamental pragmatics of living (see Figure 8). Baltes and other researchers have operationalized wisdom in a variety of ways (e.g. responses to vignettes about life problems) with wiser responses viewed as less unidimensional and more cognizant of differing circumstances and possible outcomes. Better performance on wisdom-related tasks is associated with higher levels of intelligence, creativity, and social intelligence, and is also related to social and personality styles. Wisdom is generally considered to be a positive psychological characteristic, one that is desirable in later life, if not always associated with greater age.

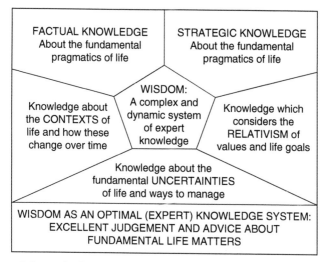

FACTUAL KNOWLEDGE
About the fundamental pragmatics of life

STRATEGIC KNOWLEDGE
About the fundamental pragmatics of life

Knowledge about the CONTEXTS of life and how these change over time

WISDOM: A complex and dynamic system of expert knowledge

Knowledge which considers the RELATIVISM of values and life goals

Knowledge about the fundamental UNCERTAINTIES of life and ways to manage

WISDOM AS AN OPTIMAL (EXPERT) KNOWLEDGE SYSTEM: EXCELLENT JUDGEMENT AND ADVICE ABOUT FUNDAMENTAL LIFE MATTERS

8. Baltes and colleagues' conceptualization of wisdom.

Thus we can see the many interwoven strands of ageing research that are exploring positive ways to age and be older. Attention here is paid to the contributions of the environment, lifestyle factors, meaning and engagement in life, resilience, and wisdom, with support successfully moving through the latter stages of life. This work continues to reveal new dimensions related to positive ageing, and provides motivation to push the boundaries of how we can age with grace. Such innovations in ageing research are the focus of the final chapter.

Chapter 6
Reflections on ageing and future directions

> Everyone is the age of their heart.
> (Guatemalan proverb)

A wide range of topics and various theories, policy frameworks, and research on ageing from historical, demographic, biological, psychological, and social perspectives have been explored in these pages. And yet the topic of ageing is so broad, and research and knowledge in the field of gerontology and related areas growing at such a pace, than any brief introduction to the topic must of necessity be incomplete. Moreover, because so many disciplines and avenues of both research and commercial and government action are taking place in this ageing space, developments are occurring at a pace never before seen.

In this final section, consideration of some of these new directions in research and clinical practice in geriatrics, along with a consideration and reflection on topics of perennial interest with respect to ageing, will be covered. These include exciting developments in healthcare and technology, as well as a consideration of what we are learning from the growing number of supercentenarian studies. The very end of life, with attendant fears about death and dying, as well as positive gains to potentially be made through cognitive training and other 'brain games', are also considered.

Healthcare frontiers

The increase in the percentage of older persons in the population has sparked fears of increasing healthcare rationing and unmet needs. Although these issues remain a reality, healthcare advances are also beginning to make inroads into disability and burden later in life. A series of studies have reported greater improvements in disability-free life expectancy than in life expectancy overall, as well as more people living to a later age with only moderate, rather than severe, disabilities. Early diagnosis, improved treatment, and amelioration of common diseases, particularly advances in chronic disease care, rendering the diseases less disabling, partially explains these trends. Other societal factors, such as the rising use of assistive technology, changes in social policies, and shifting social perceptions of disability may also contribute to this picture. Finally, improved diagnosis and interventions earlier in life, and improved living conditions in later life, probably also have a role here. Such research offers a glimpse of a future where the mantra of desiring not merely 'more years added to life, but more life in one's years' may increasingly become a reality.

Personalized medicine is an important healthcare trend for persons of all ages, but particularly older adults. Of course, the best healthcare, even in ancient times, was 'personalized' in the sense that the patient was treated as a unique individual in a particular context. Now that definition has been refined to include information about a person's genome (all of a person's genes rather than a single gene), their family history, as well as their environment, to prevent, diagnose, and treat diseases. Many branches of medicine are making advances in diagnosis and treatment by taking a more holistic approach to considering the interplay of genomics, the environment, and epigenetic variables. Cancer prevention and management is one area of medicine where the use of pre-symptomatic genetic testing and intervention approaches targeted to the genetic profiles of specific tumours has been advancing for decades. Research examining individuals at high genomic risk for Alzheimer's disease can begin testing individuals cognitively, even before symptoms manifest, and also to test the impact of a range of intervention strategies.

However, for now, with increased longevity come questions about how best to care for our oldest old. Aged care has been the subject of much negative media. Several promising models of nursing-home care have resulted in small revolutions in the industry. The model of Green House nursing homes in the USA and Small Group Living homes in the Netherlands have changed the aged care experience for residents and their families as well as professional caregivers. These new designs simultaneously tackle care delivery enhancement as well as safeguarding against staff burnout and so-called 'care-fatigue'. They emphasize personalized, patient-centred care, a home-like, supportive environment, and a sense of agency for patients, staff, and families. And we have of course already mentioned the dementia village in the Netherlands, an example of which is pictured in Figure 9. Such innovative

9. Dementia village scene.

conceptualizations of what is possible when living with dementia have also filtered into communities, where local businesses, for example, undertake training in how to be a 'dementia friendly' establishment.

Another alternative model to institutional supported living in later life is the Beacon Hill Village model, which originated in Boston, Massachusetts. Beacon Hill and other 'villages' modelled on this concept help older residents living in their own homes and neighbourhoods band together in a member-driven model to organize programmes and services. This helps to leverage existing infrastructure, transportation networks, and social and community ties. It also engenders a sense of agency and self-efficacy—people taking care of themselves (and each other) rather than being 'taken care of' by others. This movement has expanded to many other cities in the US and abroad, forming a 'village to village' network sharing ideas, processes, and governance.

Training issues are an important consideration now and into the future, in aged care but also in healthcare environments more generally. The overall geriatric health and mental health workforce will fall far short of care needs in the future, given global demographic shifts. And this is true in both the developing and the developed world. Barriers limiting training in either research and/or clinical skills in working with older people include the failure of such training programmes in health and mental health fields to provide adequate didactic content within coursework as well as a failure to develop suitable clinical placement opportunities.

Technological frontiers

Many types of technology, including web-based innovations, are having a positive impact on ageing. These run the gamut from apps for everything from helping people with dementia stay creative to medication-tracking apps and even apps to assist with navigation on hand held devices, such as enabling higher contrast viewing and large button navigation features on other apps. A specialized camera, SenseCam, is worn around the neck of persons with dementia and automatically takes low resolution photos every thirty seconds. This jogs the memory, allowing recall of events even up to many weeks in the past. These images can be edited and stored for later sharing with family, promoting social interaction. Technology also affords increased connectivity options, with grandparents for example having opportunities to connect with grandchildren on voice over internet protocol (VOIP) programmes such as Skype or via social media sites such as Facebook.

One area of technological development is helping innovate care delivered to older patients: age-specialized healthcare settings. This will in part encompass rethinking how healthcare services are organized and delivered, with geriatric surgical centres and emergency rooms already in place. Staff in such settings undergo specialized training, and the environment, instruments, tests performed, and interventions used are all designed specifically with older adults in mind, to translate into practice what is known about best standards of geriatric care.

Another area of technological innovation is the creation of personal telehealth ecosystems. Such e-health systems span home healthcare as well as acute and long-term care settings, and can marshal the expertise of a range of healthcare practitioners and specialists, optimizing care regardless of geographical distances from services and providers. A number of barriers, including technological, legal, regulatory, and financial, remain. Integrating such technological solutions along with the support and care of family members can also be a challenge. Yet enthusiasm for such approaches is growing in line with improvements in technology, as well as people of all ages embracing the increased accessibility of personal data and personalized internet-based healthcare services.

Technology to enhance functionality has improved such areas as mobility, and robots of the future are already being designed to enhance our social and emotional needs in later life. Social media platforms such as Facebook have older adults as their fastest growing user group, as has been mentioned. Studies examining the social benefits for older adults of using the internet, both to remain connected to friends and family and to reach out to new groups and acquire learning and knowledge, demonstrate some positive results. Some studies have shown greater gains in terms of mental health and decreases in social isolation from face-to-face, as opposed to electronic, means of communication. However, with increased mobility in our society, and with subsequent generations' greater ease and familiarity with the web and other technologies, this difference may well reflect a cohort effect for the most part.

Technological developments in robotics have had an impact on residential aged care. Such robots are in use in nursing homes to assist with personal care (for example, devices to lift patients) as well as robotic animals to offer stimulation. Paro, a robotic seal developed in Japan, has been the focus of much research internationally, particularly for patients with dementia who suffer severe behavioural disturbance or profound apathy. Paro is one of a range of robotic animals (which includes dinosaurs!) that act to stimulate, engage, and interact with older persons. In preliminary trials, use of Paro has reduced agitation and stimulated positive social interactions between caregivers and patients in such settings (Figure 10). And in many countries, robots assist in the delivery of telehealthcare (e.g. processing simple biological test data, such as blood pressure results; and providing a communication channel between older persons living in remote settings and health professionals), which has provided positive benefits to health and autonomy for these individuals.

An unexpected benefit of increasing technology and a shift from jobs requiring strength and manual labour to those requiring

10. Paro the seal in action.

knowledge and social skills is that older adults are increasingly able to continue to contribute to the economy for longer. If older adults remain in the workforce longer, even or perhaps especially if in part-time work, this could open up more part-time opportunities for younger people. The possibilities for job sharing between younger and older persons would also expand valuable mentoring and cross-knowledge sharing (including both explicit and tacit knowledge, and historical perspectives) between the generations. Such opportunities will only expand with the ability to work from a remote location. And if the trend towards part-time work and a longer working life were to continue, it could encourage the redistribution of leisure time and work more evenly across the lifespan, with health and well-being benefits for all generations.

Cognitive training to enhance brain power

Cognitive stimulation can potentially assist with declines in memory. In a famous series of studies, relatively 'old' rats who had been raised in a somewhat stark environment were split into two groups—one continued as they were, while the other group was placed in a more stimulating, enriched environment (lots of colours and objects to interact with). After a few months, the animals' lives were terminated and their brains examined—the rats that had lived the remainder of their lives in an enriched environment showed cortical thickening, and their brains were found to weigh more than those of their counterparts in the starker conditions. This was found to be due to several factors including increased connective networks between the neurons in their brains. This and similar research has spurred a search for ways that older humans can benefit from exercising their brains.

Enhancement strategies for optimal brain functioning include the potentially over-hyped promise of so-called 'brain games' along with more proven strategies to help combat normal age-related cognitive declines, particularly in memory. To date, the largest randomized clinical trial of cognitive training with older adults is the ACTIVE study, involving training on memory, reasoning, and speed of processing skills. Positive training effects were shown to continue for as much as five years after the training sessions had been completed, and some positive effects of this training on activities of daily living, including driving, have emerged. Such empirically validated cognitive training programmes could help improve the ability to maintain independence in later life.

Cognitive stimulation and 'brain games' have become hugely popular recently as a way to enhance memory and general cognitive functioning, with the potential to slow down deterioration in thinking due to normal age-related changes in the brain as well as diseases such as dementia. Cognitive stimulation derived from such varied activities as crossword puzzles, brain games played on computers, and even having had a cognitively stimulating job earlier in life, has been shown to have some positive effects on cognitive functioning in later life. For many of these interventions, a major challenge has been minimal generalizing of skills beyond the narrow range learned in the contexts of such games or activities, along with lack of empirical evidence for the effectiveness of many of these interventions. Newer research has shown promising evidence for such games to positively impact emotional well-being, with some reports of greater generalization to everyday contexts, but more research in this area is required. This research also builds on existing research on the positive effects of any new learning (e.g. learning a language, to play a musical instrument, and so forth) on cognitive functioning.

Supercentenarian studies

By 2050, there will be one million centenarians in the USA, and numbers of centenarians and supercentenarians (individuals over age 100 and 110, respectively) are rising across the developed and the developing world. Centenarian and supercentenarian studies provide increasing insights into function and well-being in very advanced old age. Research has shown that 30–40 per cent of a contemporary cohort of nonagenarians is independent from age 92–100 years. In a comparable study of thirty-two US supercentenarians (aged 110–19 years), about 40 per cent of participants needed minimal assistance or were independent, implying that supercentenarians are not more disabled than people in their ninth decade. Such studies do not paint a picture of the fourth age as one of inevitable dependence and poor quality of life.

Centenarian studies have demonstrated that older persons who live to age 90 and beyond are more resistant to diseases that result in disability and death at younger ages—this is known as the *selective survival effect*. Older men in these studies are also for the most part in better physical and mental health than older women; this is partially explained by the fact that men with disabling conditions, including dementia, tend to die at relatively younger ages than women. Both men and women who reach age 100 tended to still be living independently through their 90s, an example of the *compression of morbidity paradigm*, where decline and disability comes on rapidly and only just before death.

The combination of genes and environment definitely influences longevity later in life. Siblings of centenarians are eight to seventeen times more likely to reach 100 themselves. About 25–30 per cent of longevity is dependent on genetics, the rest on environment. But epigenetics is blurring these boundaries, and several studies have shown individuals living past age 90 with as many genes that put them at risk for illnesses such as cardiovascular disease and cancer as have those who do not survive. More research is needed to unravel these puzzles.

Death and dying

Death, how it is viewed, and what the rituals and ceremonies surrounding death entail differ enormously between cultures, religions, cohorts, and historical eras. Worthy of a book in itself, death has in one sense remained constant throughout history and across all peoples as an inevitable end point to life. Variations in the response to dying, and rituals surrounding death, reflect the heterogeneity of humanity itself, particularly in later life. As already mentioned, approaching death sharpens one's desire to make meaningful use of the time remaining. Older adults' resilience in the face of many adverse circumstances extends to death and dying, as research has shown that older persons for the most part cope better with the death of a partner than do younger cohorts, most likely in part because death is more expected in older age, when better social support networks are generally in place to support the bereaved. Social support networks for the bereaved are less strong, however, in cases of suicide or the death of a child, both of which are cases carrying more social stigma, which usually results in less social support being forthcoming.

Death is inevitable, and as Shakespeare opined in Hamlet, 'All that live must die, passing through nature to eternity.' The question of how one wishes the end of life to come is one that, like many aspects of ageing, has been of interest to people across the ages. Most surveys reveal people wish to die in their sleep, to not be alone, and to not be in pain. Conversely, with the advances in medical treatments prolonging life for increasing numbers of people who have suffered a variety of injuries or illnesses, the prospect of living for prolonged periods with decreased quality of life has become a concern.

Many social issues in ageing stir much debate and emotion, but perhaps none so much as the subject of assisted suicide and legalizing the choice to end one's life. With medicine's constantly expanding facility to extend life and the increasing potential for individuals to be enabled to live longer with disability and ill-health, debates have grown about the moral and ethical issues around assisted suicide—the right to end one's life has become the ever more frequent subject of legislation, research, and media reporting and speculation globally. The advancing of the Baby Boomer cohort into later life stages may well alter the content as well as the framing of such social questions.

Since 2002, the Netherlands has been able to offer legalized, physician-assisted suicide, and much societal debate as well as research has come from this nation. Research on rates of physician-assisted suicide in the Netherlands has not found large increases in persons pursuing this course of action, and physicians themselves report that regulation and public control of physician-assisted suicide has improved their confidence in the legality of their actions, contributing to an increase in the care with which life-terminating acts are approached. The Euthanasia Act of the Netherlands requires the physician to assess whether a patient's request to end their life is voluntary and well-considered; whether the patient's suffering is indeed unbearable and hopeless; whether the patient has been fully informed about their situation and, importantly, their prospects; and, finally, whether there are no reasonable alternatives to the ending of life yet to be considered. Once these questions have been fully explored, if the patient still wishes to end their life, the Act requires that another independent physician should then also be consulted. Finally, if the termination of life is still being sought, it is required to be performed with due medical care and attention. In the Netherlands, a recent study found that only a minority of patients request euthanasia at the end of life, and of these requests a majority are not granted. While other nations have enacted similar regulations, most of these have been short-lived (for example, in the Northern Territory of Australia). Currently, physician-assisted suicide is legal only in the Netherlands, Belgium, Colombia, and Luxembourg, while assisted suicide is legal in Switzerland, Germany, Japan, Albania, and in the US states of California, Oregon, Vermont, and Washington.

Are there other ways to frame questions around taking control at the end of life? 'Advanced directives' are legal documents that allow individuals to specify end of life care in advance. A living will is a type of advanced directive that spells out how the person wants their care to proceed at the end of life. In such documents various healthcare scenarios might be explored, such as when resuscitation should and should not be pursued. In the case where one is unable to speak for oneself, others can be nominated to carry out one's wishes. Healthcare power of attorney or a healthcare proxy is an individual named and empowered to legally make decisions on the part of a patient who is incapacitated.

In the United States, an initiative created by the non-profit organization Aging with Dignity has expanded what is traditionally covered in such advanced directives. The 'Five Wishes' document was introduced originally in Florida, combining a living will with healthcare power of attorney. This was seen as an innovation because it not only includes questions that are usually covered in the two existing documents (in Wishes

1 and 2) but it offers an expansion into other areas people considering their end of life experience will commonly think about—how they would want to feel in terms of physical (dis)comfort, and what thoughts and reflections they would want to have considered around the time of their death. The Five Wishes are:

Wish 1: The person I want to make decisions for me when I can't
[here the healthcare proxy is named]

Wish 2: The kind of medical treatment I want or don't want
[here what sorts of life support treatment are desired or not desired are spelled out]

Wish 3: How comfortable I want to be
[here pain management and other specifications about self-care in the last stages of life are described, including options for palliative care]

Wish 4: How I want people to treat me
[here specific wishes for being with others, whether one wishes to be at home, or with particular people or animal companions, are specified]

Wish 5: What I want my loved ones to know
[here final arrangements, such as funeral plans, as well as other matters, such as specifying forgiveness for past incidents, how one would like to be remembered, and so forth, are delineated]

The Five Wishes is part legal document and part blueprint for a conversation that many people find difficult to have. Often older adults try to initiate such conversations about end of life wishes with their children. Sometimes their efforts are rebuked, or the conversations are shut down with implicit or explicit suggestions that to talk about such matters is not desirable. But with increasing age, the realization that one is facing the end of life often provokes reflection and action. Some of this is actually creative and generative, as discussed earlier in the context of Gene Cohen's life stages. At other times a person who is facing illness and uncertainty strongly desires to have their wishes acknowledged.

The Five Wishes document contains examples of what a person might wish for under each question. For example, under Wish 3 an example wish is having enough medication given to relieve pain, even if the result is being a bit drowsy. The document has been criticized for lack of nuance between 'care' and 'treatment'; for wittingly or unwittingly encouraging euthanasia; or for its religious undertones (e.g. having people pray for you is an example given under Wish 4).

Such a list of wishes could be expanded into a broader document detailing the larger worldview and values of the older person. In this respect it would resemble the personal history documentation that many nursing homes scramble to complete when admitting new patients. The best of these ask simple but important questions about preferences in everything from food and drink to music, communication, and recreation. But in such documents the personal view of the older adult is often missing. What about all of the idiosyncratic variables—individual preferences, habits, and quirks—that make up a unique and meaningful life as well as the larger contexts—values deeply held, or relationships past or present that are defining and important? It is difficult to sum up the biological, psychosocial, emotional, and societal context of an individual's life, particularly if it has been a long and rich life. A set of wishes may be a starting point for a conversation about later life, but such wishes are most meaningful when set in the context of a person's own history, values, relationships, and experiences.

Final thoughts

Older adults are reaching out in myriad ways in our society, not only about their personal desires around the end of their own life, but also about how they want to contribute to their families, communities, and society more generally. Not only at the end of life, but throughout the course of their ageing, we should hear the wishes, and the voices, of older people.

Ageing is a process that brings gains and losses over the course of the lifespan. Ageing and later life are best viewed from a lifespan perspective, of older persons as having been shaped by the passage of their earlier years. In the face of lengthening lifespans, people are concerned about whether they will have the ability to continue to pursue their goals and meet new challenges. Understanding the process of ageing is important for individuals—but also for societies and nations—if the potential of those entering later life is to be realized.

References

Chapter 1: Ageing, a brief history

Busse, E.W. (1996). The myth, history, and science of aging.
In D.G. Blazer (ed.), *The American Psychiatric Press Textbook of Geriatric Psychiatry*. Washington, DC: American Psychiatric Press.

Classen, A. (ed.) (2007). *Old Age in the Middle Ages and the Renaissance: Interdisciplinary Approaches to a Neglected Topic*. Berlin, DE: Walter de Gruyter.

Cohen, B. and Menken, J. (2006). *Aging in Sub-Saharan Africa: Recommendations for Furthering Research*. Washington, DC: The National Academies Press.

Eggleston, K. and Tuljapurkar, S. (2011). *Aging Asia: The Economic and Social Implications of Rapid Demographic Change in China, Japan, and South Korea*. Palo Alto, CA: Shorenstein Asia-Pacific Research Center.

Fairclough, H.R. (trans.) (1926). *Horace: Satires, Epistles and Ars Poetica* (Loeb Classical Library, No. 194) (English and Latin Edition). Cambridge, MA: Harvard University Press.

Falconer, W.A. (trans.) (1923). *Cicero: On Old Age, On Friendship, On Divination* (Loeb Classical Library, No. 154). Cambridge, MA: Harvard University Press.

Kinsella, K. and He, W. (2008/2009). *An Aging World: 2008*. Washington, DC: National Institute on Aging and U.S. Census Bureau.

Lee, Desmond (trans.) (2007). *Plato: The Republic*, 3rd Edition (London: Penguin Classics).

Parkin, T.G. (2003). *Old Age in the Roman World A Cultural and Social History*. Baltimore, MD: The Johns Hopkins University Press.

Payne, T. (2015). *The Ancient Art of Growing Old*. London: Vintage Books.

Thane, P. (2010). *A History of Old Age*. Los Angeles, CA: Getty Museum.

Chapter 2: Physical and biological aspects of ageing

Christensen, K., Doblhammer, G., Rau, R., and Vaupel, J.W. (2009). Ageing populations: the challenges ahead. *Lancet* 374: 1196–208.

Davidovic, M., Sevo, G., Svorcan, P., Milosevic, D.P., Despotovic, N., and Erceg, P. (2010). Old age as a privilege of the 'selfish ones'. *Aging and Disease* 1(2): 139–46.

Evert, J., Lawler, E., Bogan, H., and Perls, T. (2003). Morbidity profiles of centenarians: survivors, delayers, escapers. *Journals of Gerontology: Medical Sciences* 58A(3): 232–7.

Jin, K. (2010). Modern biological theories of aging. *Aging and Disease* 1(2): 72–4.

Moskalev, A.A., Aliper, A.M., Smit-McBride, Z., Buzdin, A., and Zhavoronkov, A. (2014). Genetics and epigenetics of aging and longevity. *Cell Cycle* 13(7): 1063–77. doi.org/10.4161/cc.28433

Murray, S.A., Kendall, M., Boyd, K., and Sheikh, A. (2005). Illness trajectories and palliative care. *British Medical Journal* 330(7498): 1007–11.

Chapter 3: The psychology of ageing

Carstensen, Laura L., Isaacowitz, Derek M., and Charles, Susan T. (1999). Taking time seriously: a theory of socioemotional selectivity. *American Psychologist* 54(3): 165.

Charles, S. and Carstensen, L.L. (2010). Social and emotional aging. *Annual Review of Psychology* 61: 383–409.

Freund, A.M. and Baltes, P.B. (1998). Selection, optimization, and compensation as strategies of life management: correlations with subjective indicators of successful aging. *Psychology and Aging* 13(4): 531–43.

Haslam, S.A., Jetten, J., Postmes, T., and Haslam, C. (2009). Social identity, health and well-being: an emerging agenda for applied psychology. *Applied Psychology* 58(1): 1–23.

Knight, B.G. and Pachana, N.A. (2015). *Psychological Assessment and Therapy with Older Adults*. Oxford: Oxford University Press.

Roberts, B.W. and Mroczek, D. (2008). Personality trait change in adulthood. *Current Directions in Psychological Science* 17(1): 31–5.

Chapter 4: Social and interpersonal aspects of ageing

Barusch, A.S. (2008). *Love Stories of Later Life: A Narrative Approach to Understanding Romance*. New York: Oxford University Press.

Cruikshank, M. (2003). *Learning to be Old: Gender, Culture, and Aging*. Lanham, MD: Rowman & Littlefield Publishers.

Harvard School of Public Health/MetLife Foundation. (2004). *Reinventing Aging: Baby Boomers and Civic Engagement*. Boston, MA: Harvard School of Public Health, Center for Health Communication.

HelpAge International. (2011). *Insights on Ageing: A Survey Report*. London: HelpAge International.

Löfqvist, C., Granbom, M., Himmelsbach, I., Iwarsson, S., Oswald, F., and Haak, M. (2013). Voices on relocation and aging in place in very old age: a complex and ambivalent matter. *The Gerontologist* 53: 919–27.

Malpes, P.J., Mitchell, K., and Johnson, M.H. (2012). 'I wouldn't want to become a nuisance under any circumstances'—a qualitative study of the reasons some healthy older individuals support medical practices that hasten death. *New Zealand Medical Journal* 125(1358): 9–19.

United Nations Development Programme. (2014). *Human Development Report 2014. Sustaining Human Progress: Reducing Vulnerabilities and Building Resilience*. New York: United Nations Development Programme.

UNFPA (United Nations Population Fund) and HelpAge International. (2012). *Ageing in the Twenty-First Century: A Celebration and a Challenge*. New York and London: UNFPA and HelpAge.

WHO. (2007). *Women, Ageing and Health: A Framework for Action.* Geneva, CH: WHO. <http://www.who.int/ageing/publications/Women-ageing-health-lowres.pdf>. Accessed 8 November 2015.

Chapter 5: Positive and successful ageing

Cohen, G.D. (2005). *The Mature Mind: The Positive Power of the Aging Brain.* New York: Basic Books.

Fernández-Ballesteros, R. (2011). Positive ageing: objective, subjective, and combined outcomes. *Electronic Journal of Applied Psychology* 7(1): 22–30.

Geiger, P.J., Boggero, I.A., Brake, C.A., Caldera, C.A., Combs, H.L., Peters, J.R., and Baer, R.A. (2015). Mindfulness-based interventions for older adults: a review of the effects on physical and emotional well-being. *Mindfulness* [e-print ahead of publication]. doi: 10.1007/s12671-015-0444-1

Jeste, D. et al. (2013). Association between older age and more successful aging: critical role of resilience and depression. *American Journal of Psychiatry* 170(2): 188–96.

Karp, A., Paillard-Borg, S., Wang, H.X., Silverstein, M., Winblad, B., and Fratigliono, L. (2006). Mental, physical and social components in leisure activities equally contribute to decrease dementia risk. *Dementia and Geriatric Cognitive Disorders* 21(2): 65–73.

Levy, B. and Langer, E. (1994). Aging free from negative stereotypes: successful memory in China and among the American deaf. *Journal of Personality and Social Psychology* 66: 989–97.

National Health and Medical Research Council (NH&MRC). (1996). *Promoting the Health of Indigenous Australians: A Review of Infrastructure Support for Aboriginal and Torres Strait Islander Health Advancement.* Final report and recommendations. Canberra, ACT: NHMRC.

Verghese, J., Lipton, R.B., Katz, M.J., Hall, C.B., Derby, C.A., Kuslansky, G., Ambrose, A.F., Sliwinski, M., and Buschke, H. (2003). Leisure activities and the risk of dementia in the elderly. *New England Journal of Medicine* 348: 2508–16.

WHO. (2002). *Active Aging: A Policy Framework.* Geneva, CH: WHO.

WHO. (2007). Global age-friendly cities: a guide. Geneva, CH: WHO. <http://apps.who.int/iris/bitstream/10665/43755/1/9789241547307_eng.pdf>. Accessed 8 November 2015.

Wild, K., Wiles, J.L., and Allen, R.E. (2013). Resilience: thoughts on
the value of the concept for critical gerontology. *Ageing & Society*
33(1): 137–58.

Chapter 6: Reflections on ageing and future directions

Christensen, K., Doblhammer, G., Rau, R., and Vaupel, J.W. (2009).
Ageing populations: the challenges ahead. *Lancet* 374: 1196–208.

Hwang, U. and Morrison, R.S. (2007). The geriatric emergency
department. *JAGS* 55: 1873–6.

Onwuteaka-Philipsen, B.D., Rurup, M.L., Pasman, H.R., and van der
Heide, A. (2010). The last phase of life: who requests and receives
euthanasia or physician-assisted suicide? *Medical Care*
48(7): 596–603.

Tamura, T., Yonemitsu, S., Itoh, A., Oikawa, D., Kawakami, A.,
Higashi, Y., Fujimoto, T., and Nakajima, K. (2004). Is an
entertainment robot useful in the care of elderly people with severe
dementia? *Journal of Gerontology: Medical Sciences* 59A(1): 83–5.

Willis, S.L. et al. (2006). Long-term effects of cognitive training on
everyday functional outcomes in older adults. *JAMA* 296: 2805–14.

Further reading

Barusch, A.S. (2008). *Love Stories of Later Life: A Narrative Approach to Understanding Romance*. New York: Oxford University Press.

Buettner, D. (2012). *The Blue Zones: 9 Lessons for Living Longer from the People Who've Lived the Longest*, 2nd edn. Washington, DC: National Geographic.

Carstensen, L. (2011). *A Long Bright Future*. New York: Public Affairs.

Cohen, G.D. (2000). *The Creative Age: Awakening Human Potential in the Second Half of Life*. New York: Quill.

Cohen, G.D. (2005). *The Mature Mind: The Positive Power of the Aging Brain*. New York: Basic Books.

Cozolino, L. (2008). *The Healthy Aging Brain: Sustaining Attachment, Attaining Wisdom*. New York: W.W. Norton & Company.

Gawande, A. (2014). *Being Mortal: Illness, Medicine, and What Matters in the End*. London: Profile Books.

Hill, R.D. (2005). *Positive Aging*. New York: W.W. Norton & Company.

Moody, H.R. and Sasser, J.R. (2012). *Aging: Concepts and Controversies*. Los Angeles, CA: Sage.

Olshansky, S.J. and Carnes, B.A. (2001). *The Quest for Immortality: Science at the Frontiers of Aging*. New York: W.W. Norton & Company.

Pillemar, K. (2011). *30 Lessons for Living: Tried and True Advice from the Wisest Americans*. New York: Hudson Street Press.

Rowe, J.W. and Kahn, R.L. (1998). *Successful Aging*. New York: Dell.

Seligman, M.E.P. (2011). *Flourish*. New York: The Free Press.

Snowdon, D. (2002). *Aging with Grace: What the Nun Study Teaches Us About Leading Longer, Healthier, and More Meaningful Lives*. New York: Bantam Books.

Vaillant, G. (2002). *Aging Well: Surprising Guideposts to a Happier Life from the Landmark Harvard Study of Adult Development.* New York: Little, Brown, and Company.

Brief compendium of ageing organizations of note

Abbeyfield Housing: <https://www.abbeyfield.com/>
AARP, Inc., formerly the American Association of Retired Persons: <http://www.aarp.org/>
Aging with Dignity: <http://www.agingwithdignity.org>
Alzheimer's Disease International: <http://www.alz.co.uk/>
Beacon Hill Village: <http://www.beaconhillvillage.org/>
Compassion in Care: <http://www.compassionincare.com/>
Global Age Watch: <http://www.helpage.org/global-agewatch/>
Help Age International: <http://www.helpage.org/>
International Federation on Ageing: <http://www.ifa-fiv.org/>
US National Institute on Aging: <https://www.nia.nih.gov/>
United Nations, Aging: <http://www.un.org/en/globalissues/ageing/>
University of the Third Age (worldwide site): <http://www.worldu3a.org/>
World Health Organization (WHO), Aging: <http://www.who.int/topics/ageing/en/>

Publisher's acknowledgements

We are grateful for permission to include the following copyright material in this book.

Extract from Dylan Thomas, 'Do not go gentle into that good night', *The Collected Poems of Dylan Thomas: The New Centenary Edition*. With permission of David Higham.

The publisher and author have made every effort to trace and contact all copyright holders before publication. If notified, the publisher will be pleased to rectify any errors or omissions at the earliest opportunity.

Index

Index